Guided
BY AN
UNSEEN HAND

The Ministry Autobiography of
Haywood T. Gray

For my friend Dr Jasper Reed

Be faithful!

Haywood

HAYWOOD T. GRAY

Lulu Publishing Services rev. date: 10/31/2016

DEDICATION

This book is dedicated to the blessed memories of
The Late Reverend J. W. Brown and
The Late Reverend Dr. Eugene Burns Turner

and in honor of
The Reverend Dr. Arthur R. White

Fathers in Ministry, Examples in Life, and
Shoulders On Which I Have Leaned

TABLE OF CONTENTS

FOREWORD

WHEN I WAS asked to write the foreword for this book, though flattered for being asked, at first I was intimidated. I have never written a foreword before. I wanted to say no, but because of my love and admiration for the writer and my commitment to younger ministers, I had to say "yes." and how glad I am that I did!

The first thing I told the author when he asked me to do this is that I am a slow reader and reading the book will take me some time. How wrong I was. Once I got started reading about "the store," "the Sunday School," "the marble matches," "the choir rehearsals," and "the call to ministry," I could hardly put the manuscript down. I read the entire book in a matter of hours. It is invigorating. It is awesome. It is transforming.

Rarely does anyone lay himself or his life open to public scrutiny with such openness and honesty as this author does. His style is simple. His message is clear. His spirit is genuine. He reveals his own limitations with the same completeness as he reports his accomplishments. His extreme personal modesty is evident everywhere, and there is no allusion to pride or pomposity. Throughout the writing, there seems to be a compelling effort to be true to God and honest with man.

This book bares the heart, soul, strength, and mind of one of God's true servant leaders whose revealed aim is to serve man and please God. The size of the writer's heart is evident everywhere in the writing by his selfless generosity. However, the true magnitude of the human heart is not determined as much by its size as it is by its shape. It is not measured so much by how much it gives but by how freely it parts with what it possesses. The self-giving and personal sacrifice of this writer is evidence that his heart is shaped like God's own heart - compassionate, generous, and selfless. The people that he has mentored, the lives that he has touched, and the ministries that he has helped to shape will form a great procession of servants bent in the direction of the divine.

The soul of the man is laid out in this book for everyone to see. Some people will read it one way and some another. I dare not presume to know how God will read it, but I venture to guess that no person or product that ever won a Pulitzer Prize, an Emmy, a Grammy, a Nobel Peace Prize or any other award will outdistance this product in purpose, passion, or power.

The strength of the writer is revealed in his willingness to lay his limitations candidly before a critical public and leave the judgment of them there. Few people in his profession, or any other for that matter, would admit publicly that they feel ill-prepared to perform the duties that their positions require. To the contrary, this writer: a preacher, a pastor, a moderator, and a denominational leader openly admits that he has never been to seminary. In this case, honesty is the best policy; for, absent the formal theological training, this writer demonstrates a greater understanding of biblical doctrine and theological application than many who have been much more formally trained will ever comprehend.

The mind of this minister is a miracle. It is born out of necessity, nurtured in experience, driven by compulsion, and honed through personal practice. Not many writers demonstrate the ability to draw from the normal and natural experiences of life such a wellspring of wisdom and convey that wisdom to others with such pertinence, conviction, clarity, and passion. This publication is truly a repository of resourcefulness, wit, and wisdom, but it also captures the intellect of the reader, finds an inquisitive nerve, aims at a worthy target, and hits the "spot" dead on. The author's keen intellect, genuine sense of humor, sincere commitment to ministry, and profound reservoir of knowledge all come to the fore in this writing. Yet, these neither blunt nor abort the purpose of the publication which is to pass on to others insight and encouragement to do Christian ministry and to do it well.

This book demonstrates that this writer has done this in a way that distinguishes him as a true servant of God, committed without reservation to His cause and Kingdom. His compassion is uniquely demonstrated by his "divinely created" family. His generosity is displayed through multiple instances in which he shares with others and gives away what could perhaps be better used by himself. His keen sensitivity is clearly shown through the many acts of kindness that both complement and satisfy his own needs as he ministers to the needs of others. He exemplifies the herculean strength to carry burdens alone that would ordinarily be too heavy for many people to carry with the aid of others. And there is no question about his intrepid faith which is bold enough to debate with God yet stubborn enough never to abandon or forsake Him, while, at the same time, enduring and overcoming immense pain.

The ultimate aim in the life of this author, the main goal of his ministry, and the central focus of his purpose are all summarized in his statement found in the last paragraph of chapter two. There these words are recorded: "If l can be faithful at ministry and if I can keep the vows that I have made with God and if I can serve without reservation, one day I can expect that the One Who caught me in my collar and gave me His assignment will hold the door [of heaven] open for me. The sky will split, the clouds will part, the atmosphere will break and the Lord shall descend. The dead in Christ will rise and those who remain will be caught up. When the saints go marching in through the doors to eternity which our Lord will have opened for us, hearing the welcome voice of Jesus saying 'well done' will more than compensate for every tear, every perceived snub and every unacknowledged act of service. For that possibility, I am happy to hold the door open for others."

To the writer I say "right on." When God gathers us in glory and graces us with His divine judgment, I dare say that He is not going to ask how many sermons did you preach, or how many weddings did you perform, or how many meetings did you attend, or how much energy did you expend, or how much rhetoric did you employ, but how many lives did you touch, and how many minds did you change, and how many steps did you alter, and how many hearts did you challenge and bend in the direction of God? When it comes Haywood's time to respond, the answer has to be uncertain only because the number will be unknown and unknowing, as the entities will be innumerable. Consequently, I believe that God's ultimate response will be, "Enter thou into the joy of your Lord."

To the reader I say, read to your pleasure; read to your benefit; read until your heart is happy and your soul is satisfied. Then you can come and join me and we can go together and say, Thank you, Haywood, for this blessing from God and thank you, God, for your blessing to us in Haywood T. Gray!

Friend, colleague and grateful beneficiary,
James Donald Ballard
October 15, 2014

PREFACE

THIS YEAR MARKS my fortieth year in ministry and it occurred to me that very few people know the story of my ministry. I have been very private about both my personal life and my public ministry choosing to share very little of the ingredients in my recipes for my life and ministry. One reason has been the simple fact that people really do not like to hear others who talk too much about themselves. It is also true that, for a very long time, I have thought of my journey in ministry to have been nothing more than ordinary. However, as I become more reflective in this season of my life and service, I am struck by the fact that my journey in life has been nothing akin to ordinary.

I am not sure what the retelling of these stories will do for those who will read them. I am uncertain that they will prove to be the good fodder for a learning experience for anyone who reads these pages. I have never thought myself to be a teacher. I hope that some person in the morning of ministry will heed to my cautions and not make the same mistakes I made. I hope that these "old school" tales will interest some "new breed" minister and equip that minister with the timeless tools for ministry and service. I hope that this collection of my musing about the past of four decades will help shape my focus for the final years of ministry ahead of me.

I have never thought that my experiences in ministry have been especially interesting. For the most part, many of these experiences have never been told before. They do come from an imperfect perspective that being my own. They are the results of my remembering many years hence. They are only a part of my life story. However, they are what I felt, what I thought, and how I reasoned for the place I was in life and ministry. As such, these accounts should not be considered a guide for others nor should they be merely dismissed as one person's coping and struggle in ministry. They should be seen for what they are: vignettes from a long ministry held together by the threads of fierce desire to serve God faithfully.

I have come to this writing because I am becoming more and more aware that my current work as a denominational executive will likely be my last place and position of ministry. I will likely never pastor a Church again. The dynamic duo of old age and failing health will block my lifelong dream of practicing ministry in an academic setting. I have come to that time in life when one becomes concerned about the legacy one will leave. Perhaps for me the writing of this book is a necessary exercise to help me shape the contours of the phase of ministry into which I am now entering. The best way forward comes after taking a thoughtful look back.

I am extremely grateful to the many persons that God has sent to add value to my life and ministry. They have been both the great and the small, the famous and the unknown, the conservative and the outlandish. Each has poured something into my life and they have allowed me to drink deeply from the well of their wisdom and friendship and support. Many of their names will appear on the pages that follow and I trust that they will see their inclusion in this book as another expression of my gratitude for them and for what they have meant for me.

It is also true that I cannot tell my story without bringing others into this retelling. In those circumstances where my telling how their lives intersected with mine may not protect their privacy, I have used pseudonyms. I have, by in large, sought to be true to my recollections and as complete as I could possibly be. Yet propriety demands some gaps and some things to be left unsaid.

I struggled a while to find an apt title for these pages held together more by memory than by reason. The things that I have chosen to say and the years that I completely skipped are inexplicable. I don't know why some memories remain clear and others are as the sun trying to peep through a cloudy day. The more that I worked on the pages, the more I wished that I had developed the habit of journaling.

But there was a common denominator in the stories I retell herein. In each story, in each remembrance, in each detail shared on these pages, I can clearly see how my life was guided. Looking back, it is almost as if my life has followed some route and I have only needed to adhere to the road signs on this journey. Whether I turned left or right, speeded forward or threw it quickly into reverse, I could always feel the presence of a Hand turning me this way or that way, touching my heart, and bringing nourishment for my soul. The Hand has been unseen, but Its presence unmistakable. Without question, my life has been guided by an unseen Hand.

I sat with my youngest son, Allen, some time ago. We were having a lighthearted moment about what he and his brothers should have engraved on my tombstone. He, in his ever joking way, asked that I make the tombstone expression brief with few letters so that it would not cost them so much. What was a joke later became a serious consideration for me. What really should be inscribed on my tombstone? I begin to seriously ponder what might go on that granite stone when my time comes. "Executive Secretary-Treasurer of the General Baptist State Convention of North Carolina" would break the bank with the children and appear far too grandiose. "Pastor, Denominational Leader, Christian Statesman" sounds too formal and much too contrived. I thought about "Preacher" or "Writer" or "Scholar", but I had to admit I am probably not that good at either of those to immortalize it on a grave marker. I finally settled on two words and an ellipsis: "He loved . . ."

The pages that follow tell of the people and places I loved, the work and witness I loved, and the struggles and victories I loved. For the truth is that I loved my calling and purpose in life. I loved being able to love people from this avenue of service. And may it also give rise to the certain truths I learned about the God I love and who loves me so.

Haywood T. Gray
Raleigh, NC
August 21, 2016

CHAPTER 1

"AND I FELT BRAND NEW"

I HOPE NEVER TO forget the third Thursday night in August 1969. That was the night that I was converted. Converted seems a rather harsh word to use to describe a nine-year-old who made the decision to join the Church. However, that was the acceptable language of the third week of August. The Mars Hill Baptist Church of Capron, Virginia would hold its annual revival that week with the well-known objective of getting sinners "converted" and coming to the "mourner's bench." The late Reverend Raymond L. Lassiter, Sr. was our pastor and each year he would bring some fiery preacher to our pulpit for revival. Being nine meant I didn't share very much excitement about the renowned preacher or about how many people would come to the mourner's bench that week. For me, it was more about having something to do and a chance to sit with my friends from school on the last pew and, when not in the view of the adult who had been assigned to discipline that back pew, pass notes and giggle at what was going on around us.

It happens that the Mars Hill Church was located right next door to the local juke joint. In those days, we called them "piccolo" joints. It was there that the young gathered to drop coins in the jukebox on weekend nights to hear the latest grooves and dance much too close and much too long with each other. It was also well known that spirits (and not the kind of which a proper Christian should partake) were sold out of the back room. In the summer, a loudspeaker placed on the outside made the place crawl with young (as well as some not-so-young) people all summer long.

Mr. R. C. was known only as "Dick" to everyone everywhere, (I thought). He was the proprietor of the establishment known locally as the place to be. It never had a name so we just called it "The Store," but everyone seemed to have known that it was there. Mr. C hired my grandmother as his complete staff. She did whatever had to be done around the place from selling nabs and sodas from the front room counter or washing shot glasses from the illegal bar operating from the back. With school being out for summer and there being nothing good to come from leaving a nine year at home alone, I was regularly at the "Store" with my grandmother.

For a nine-year-old, the place was the ideal play place. Mr. C, being the ultimate entrepreneur, sold just about everything one could imagine. The "Store" was part hardware store, part grocery store, part gas station, part bar and grill. He even raised hogs out back. At nine, I was at a place where I could be helpful around the place so during the days I would pump gas at thirty-three cents a gallon or stock shelves or sweep the floors. Mr. C had rigged a watering system for his hogs whereby water pumped from the well would flow through a series of gutters before emptying into their watering trough. On hot summer days, I'd pump and pump until the water overflowed the watering trough and created a "hog swimming pool." I would take great delight in watching the hogs splash and wallow in the muddy water. Between the "Store" and the Church was a grove of trees that provided numerous adventures for a kid and opposite the "Store" was the Church graveyard. This particular arrangement of lands and property provided infinite opportunity for play and imagination to take hold. I could spend hours and hours outdoors imagining myself in one adventure or another. Whether it was jumping off the back porch of the "Store," watching the hogs wallow in the summer resort I'd created for them or laying under one of the trees in the grove, it was all a paradise for me.

Things radically changed in the evenings. When the piccolo joint got to rocking at night, there was no time for play. It was work. Sometimes it was helping to pick up beer cans scattered on the ground in case the deputies came by unexpected. It could have been getting the pigs' feet from the pickled jar to allow someone to get something on his stomach before a night of hard drinking. It may have been drying the shot glasses after they had been dipped in scalding water so they would be ready for the next fifty cents paying customer. Sometimes it was watching the antics of some poor soul who had had one shot too many trying to navigate the two steps that led to the outside of the place.

Though I did not know it then, it was also a dangerous place and especially dangerous for a child. Fights often broke out when a man thought another man was looking too long and too hard at his woman. The rumor that someone had a gun would send me running to the windowless stock room while Mr. C (with his hand in his pocket) would stand as a giant sentinel at the front door. I saw far too many young people leave with a bruise or a knife wound while Motown blared on the speakers.

There was, in those days, great respect for the Church. So Mr. C would always close the piccolo joint down for revival. The selling of dry goods, gas and junk food went on, but the back room activities halted and the dance floor fell silent for the third week in August. The community went into prayer that some of the folk who had been cutting up during the second week would find their way to the mourner's bench on the third week.

Having nothing else to do, I went to revival every night that week. I cannot say that I was especially interested in Church nor was I especially

3

disinterested. It was as normal a part of our life experience as were school and home. Everybody went to Church. Of course, some more frequently than others. There were those who only made it on the obligatory high days of Easter and Mother's Day. Up until that point, my family members were fairly regular Church goers. Inasmuch as our Church only had services one day a month – on third Sundays, it is hard to not be a fairly regular attender on that cycle. Most of the people visited other Churches on the other Sundays of the month. My family, however, was content to be faithful to third Sundays.

Overall, I liked Church. The music was good and seeing people dress up was something special. Unlike most of my peers, I was also intrigued by our pastor who had a great reputation as a preacher and singer. He could move people out of their seats with the rhythm and melody of his voice. When the other children on my pew were asleep or playing with fans or hymnbooks, I could be found listening intently to Rev. Raymond L. Lassiter, Sr. preach. I wasn't as interested in his content as I was in his style.

Rev. Lassiter always put a lot into the "opening the doors of the Church" part of our monthly worship service. His invitations to discipleship were always a sincere pleading for the souls of people. Unlike his other contemporaries, I do not remember him using the Invitation to Discipleship to scare us or berate us or condemn us. I always remember him speaking so passionately about the love and forgiveness of Christ. It was in that routine of opening the doors of the Church that I learned about grace and the love of God in Christ. His invitations were always moving and powerful, but I never thought that he was talking to me.

I don't think that I really intended to go to Church every night during that week of revival, but it ended up that way. I arrived at about "preaching time" for the first few nights. It was summer and it didn't get dark until after eight. I could always find something to do at the

"Store." As darkness fell, I would make my way to the back pew, join my friends and take in whatever the night's worship had to offer.

I do not recall the visiting preacher's name nor do I remember his sermons. I do remember his cufflinks. That seems to be a small thing, but I remember he had the shiniest "things" that peeked out from under his black robe when he raised his hands. I don't think I had ever really seen cufflinks before and, after Monday night, I could not wait to get back to see those shiny "things" again. I tried on a couple of occasions to come down front and shake his hand with the ulterior motive of seeing them up close, but the press of the adults prevented me.

Though I adored his jewelry, I wasn't really impressed by the visiting minister's sermons and I was not at all impressed by his "opening the doors of the church." Unlike Rev. Lassiter who made that part of the worship service to be calm and moving, this minister made it loud and scary. Hell was waiting for everybody – little children included! That night was always the last night to make "the decision" and waiting too long meant eternal damnation. Every sin known to man and many more sins than a nine-year-old couldn't even know about was condemned. He accused somebody present of being guilty of at least one of them. A few sinners made their way down front only to have the visiting minister to yell at and cajole them. I didn't think myself one of the crowd he was screaming at and, even if I was, I would never allow myself to be humiliated in front of the people I knew.

Thursday night was different. For some reason, I went to Church early and sat through the prayer service. It was that service that changed my life. I was captivated by the prayers of the old deacons of our Church and community. I knew many of them as Mr. This or That, but never saw them in the light of being spiritual leaders in the Church. Their prayers were moving and beautiful. The rhythm and rise of their petitions to God moved the congregation. They physically bowed at their pews and called upon the name of the Lord while their bodies quaked and jerked at the ushering of the Spirit into their souls. I saw the old women – the mothers of the Church – stand to testify of the grace of God and heard their tender and soft voices tell of the "dangers, toils and snares" through which God had brought them. They were moved to tears as they told their stories and as they yielded their flesh to the Spirit.

And they sang. They sang until their words hung over us like a cloud shielding us from harm. They sang until they shed tears as if there was a washing away of the bitters of the past going on. They raised their hands neither in war nor in protest, but in a beautiful surrendering to God – a waving of the white flag. They sang until the power of the Lord came down.

I was impressed because I knew these people in a wholly different context. I knew them as farmers who had not the benefit of an education, but who could pray with an eloquence beyond Shakespeare. I knew them as reserved and stern school teachers who rarely smiled or showed emotion at school, but who would wave their hands and stomp their feet with the rhythm of the songs being sung. I knew them as quiet, soft-spoken people who, now infused with a holy boldness, spoke with a certain confidence about what God could do. I saw them transformed and I knew I wanted – somehow, someway – to have that transformation too.

Perhaps it was a part of God's plan for my life that the visiting minister did not make the altar call that Thursday night, but our pastor did. Though I had heard Rev. Lassiter's plea many times before, that particular Thursday night was the first time I realized that he could be talking to me. This love of God, this walk with Christ, this unmerited favor could all be mine. All I had to do was take hold of it and believe. Only believe.

I don't remember getting up and moving down the aisle. I just remember coming into the welcoming arms of our pastor. With a red face and tears streaming uncontrollably, I answered his simple questions. "Do you believe that Jesus is the son of God?" "Yes," I said. "Do you believe that he died for your sins and on the third day rose from the grave?" "Yes," I said. "Do you wish to be baptized and join the church?" "Yes, sir," I said. And I felt brand new.

Little did I know then, but I would return to that scene a thousand times in my mind over the course of my life. When I doubted my course or even doubted the hand of God in my life, I went back to that safe and glorious place of August 1969. When I was a pastor and a child would accept the invitation to discipleship that I was now offering following the pattern of Rev. Lassiter, I would go back to that place. When I wanted to give up, it was into Rev. Lassiter's arms that my mind and spirit would always take me where I could find renewal and courage. When life and ministry were too large for me, I could hear the echoes of a nine-year-old saying "yes" when as an adult I wanted desperately to say "no." It is as real to me today as it was now more than four decades ago.

Far too many Christians have become too far removed from their first experience with Christ. Years and tears tend to bring dark shadows that obscure one's view of that life changing experience. Once that connection to one's own personal salvation experience is lost, one loses much of the meaning and purpose which salvation brings to life. Ministers should be extremely careful to return to that starting point across the years of ministry. To go there is to affirm again the legitimacy of one's place in Christ. Having that memory serves to realign priorities and reminds us of what is really important in this life. There is strength and courage and power to be re-lived from that moment. It is a strength and courage and power that will help you in the rough times and the rough places of ministry.

A good friend of mine, The Reverend Clarence Johnson, has a sermon that he calls "Do You Remember Your Wash Day?" In it, Rev. Johnson recalls the days of old when people did their laundry on a specific day of the week using an old wash pot that sat in the yard. He makes the comparison of our conversion to a spiritual wash day and advises us never to forget that day.

I hope never to forget mine. It is my landmark when I feel lost. It is my lighthouse when the swelling tide pushes me off course. It was the first step on a wonderful journey.

Lessons for Ministry

1. Always remember and identify with your conversion. Practice remembering it. Re-tell it to yourself. Make it as clear a memory in your mind as you can. As you grow in ministry and doubts about your work and service appear, remembering your start in Christ will give you strength and affirmation.

2. Take very seriously your opportunity to "open the doors of the Church." Put effort into it. Imagine how your words sound and how people might react to it. Do not seek style in offering invitations to follow Christ; seek sincerity. Your sincerity (or lack thereof) will reflect in your words, your voice and your face.

3. I began the habit of recording the names of sermons and dates and places where I preached them in the early days of my ministry. This record started out as notes in a spiral bound notebook that had English class notes in the front and a record of preaching in the back. It evolved to a computerized spreadsheet over the years. Somewhere in moving from place to place over the years, the early handwritten record was lost, but I never lost the count. At the time of this writing, I have stood to preach over 4,100 times. After all those years and all those sermons, I

finally figured out that I was counting the wrong thing. Instead of counting the times I preached, I should have been counting the number of persons who responded to my preaching and chose Christ. That is the number that really matters.

CHAPTER 2

"I GOT A NEW NAME OVER IN ZION ... AND IT'S MINE"

I WAS BAPTIZED ON a cool, bright fall morning at the Calvary Baptist Church in Yale, Virginia. I am not sure why this decision was made other than the fact that the Calvary Church was the traditional Church of our maternal family line. The roots of that side of my family tree run deep into the soil of Sussex County, Virginia. However, I was born and bred next door in Southampton County, Virginia. I assume that the decision to have me baptized in Yale and not Capron was an effort to connect me to those roots and to follow the tradition of my grandmother's side of the family.

I do not remember much of that fall day, but I clearly recall the twenty or so minutes that it took to move through the baptism ritual. I do remember the candidates being draped in various white articles: towels, wraps, and some things nearly akin to shrouds. We were lined up and marched, single file, to the above ground, cinderblock baptism pool that stood on the side of the Church. They sang a song that I would much later learn was the obligatory baptism hymn, "Take Me to the Water." One by one, the Reverend W. A. Cotton would take our small hands and lead us into what appeared to be a sea of water for a young child. I wasn't afraid, but I do recall thinking that this was a lot of water for such a little person. I only had the vague outline of what I was consenting to. I knew that I would be a member of the Church after baptism. I knew that Jesus had been baptized. I knew that everybody I knew was happy that I was getting baptized, but that was about all I knew or that I understood. It was not that I could not understand, but it was that no one thought it important to sit me down and explain things to me. Perhaps my family thought the Church leaders would do that. Maybe the Church leaders thought my family would do that. In either case, no one did and I learned most of what I knew about the rite standing in line on that Fall Sunday morning seeing what those in line ahead of me endured. It would be much later before I came to understand the ritual and its meaning for my life. In later years as a Pastor, I would take special care to meet personally with candidates for baptism to talk about the rite, what would happen, what it meant and what would be expected of them. The fact that I would never delegate this task to others probably stems from my personal baptism experience.

I remember being told to hold my breath and close my eyes. In the excitement of the moment, I only got one of the instructions correct. I held my breath but I forgot to close my eyes. I remember going under the water for what seemed to be a very long time. I saw the colored leaves of fall floating atop the water and the Sunday morning sun shining. The experience paled in comparison to what had happened a few weeks before in the revival service, but it was a serene and meaningful event for me. It meant much because it was what Jesus had done and, more than anything else, I wanted to be like Jesus.

As the candidates dressed in white found their way back to the Church or to cars or to the outdoor facilities to change from their dripping baptismal garments, they changed their song. I can still hear their song, "I got a new name over in Zion and it's mine, it's mine, it's mine." That would be the second time in my brief nine years that I had lived that I had a new name.

Miss Anzella Claud, the local midwife, scrawled Tyrone Freeman on the paper that certified my birth on April 21, 1960. I was given my father's middle name, Haywood, as my first name, but I was never told why my mother picked Tyrone for my middle name. Freeman was her last name. Inasmuch as my mother and father were never married, I supposed I had not the right to my father's name. Most of the people who know me from home and Church know me as Tyrone, but at school and everywhere else I was known by my father's middle name, Haywood.

For some reason, my name changed between first and second grade. The now tender and yellowing pages of my report cards from that time tell the story. In Grade 1, Haywood Tyrone Freeman is written in block letters on the outside. A photograph of a cheesy grinning little fellow in a shirt and a tie is glued to the scrapbook that archives my school records. In Grade 2, the picture has radically changed to an "I'm-not-going-to-say-cheese-for-anything" kind of expression and the shirt and tie have been replaced by a pullover. The name is Haywood T. Gray. That name was written in the most beautiful script on the outside of my second grade report card. That report card also reported my receiving A's and B's in every subject except "Deportment" in which I could only muster C's. For the rest of my life, I would use that moniker and try to imitate the beautiful, fluid style of my second grade teacher in writing my name.

A name is all that I know that I received from my father. I hasten to argue that his absence in my life has never been explained and I do not blame him. I only recall seeing him a few times in my life. As a child, he was spoken of only sporadically and never with any negative context. He was an almost ghostly figure in my early life about whom I had no particular feelings. There are many possible explanations for my father's absence. I was born in an era where an out of wedlock birth was publicly shunned. In those days when paternity testing was unheard of, there were always those questions of the legitimacy of any young mother's claim of "who the father was." My maternal and paternal families were from different backgrounds and certain traditions prevented an easy mixing of the blood of these two family lines.

I do not know what support my father gave to my mother who bore me or to my grandmother who raised me. It was never discussed. I do not know which presents under the silver aluminum Christmas tree that resurrected itself every Christmas were provided by my father. It was never disclosed. I do not know what kind of man my father was nor what kind of life he lived. It was never told to me. I never recall having a conversation of any importance with my father. I do have a photograph of him, taken in the 1960's which reveal a handsome, dapper man. It is that image that I choose to remember whenever I think of him.

Thank God for the Church! More specifically, thank God for the men of our little Church in the backwoods of Southside Virginia. It was the deacons of that Church who took on the responsibility of teaching me how to maneuver through the rough waters of growing into manhood. They gave me instruction in things both big and small. They told me that you should always hold the door open for a lady. They told me to never wear a hat indoors. They taught me how to tie a tie. They took me to the barber shop on Saturday mornings and filtered the barber shop talk that I was so interested in by the ever-changing expressions on their faces. For my benefit, they smiled or grimaced at the conversation at hand as a signal to me for what was appropriate and what was inappropriate. It was to these men that I came when I didn't understand life. They helped me to make sense of it.

The role of the deacon was very different in those days. Because most pastors did not live in the communities where they pastored, the deacon was responsible for the business of the Church, the visitation of the sick, and the representation of the Church in all things local. As a result, these men cultivated large influences in the local community.

Everyone knew them and everyone came to them with their problems and concerns. To a young child, they were larger-than-life figures and I felt very special to have merited their attention and guidance.

I do not know if they mentored me because of my grandmother's asking or if they saw this as a natural extension of their role as keepers of the Church and community. Perhaps their interest in me grew out of the near prophetic predictions of the elders in my community that I was a "special" child and that God had something "special" in store for me. I do know that these deacons were chiefly responsible for my passage into young adulthood and for my concept of what real manhood was. I do not submit that these were perfect men by any measure. They bore the weight of imperfection as all men do. They aimed for perfection, but like all of us, they rarely hit the mark. Later in adulthood, I would be surprised to discover the shortcomings of these men whom I had assumed had achieved sainthood before dying. However, they carried themselves in such a way as to demand respect and earn the leadership that they assumed in our community.

In all likelihood, I am sure that I count the measure of these men beyond what they were. All heroes are larger than life in our eyes. However, my father was unknown to me and every young boy needs a hero. I worked and played around "The Store" where the only role models to be found were intoxicated men who lacked self-control or men who were abusers of women or other men who had long ago traded hope for despair. In such a context, it is easy to understand why these men of the Church were giants in my eyes. I am afraid that my life would have taken a radically different course had it not been for their intervention in my life.

It is not that I did not idolize my pastors. I did. They were the models of success (as we knew it), education (as we knew it), and influence (as we knew it). But they, like my father, were absent in my youth. Pastoral care was virtually non-existent for me and in our community. Our Church worshipped only one Sunday a month and our pastors lived elsewhere. Other than a very brief encounter (probably a pat on the head or a quick "be a good boy"), I really had no contact with a pastor when I was a child. Regardless of how good they were in the pulpit, even the best of preachers can hold the attention of a nine-year-old for only so long. The impressions that they leave are fleeting impressions at best.

The impact that these men had on my youth informed my ministry as I have always sought opportunity to be role models and coaches for young, African-American men. Though different in context, the fact that many African-American males are growing up without the benefit of a father in the home has not very much changed from what it was when I was a child. Having never forgotten what the deacons of my home Church did for me, I always sought to make looking out for young men a priority in my ministry.

I came to my first official pastorate when I was twenty years old. As such, it was easy for me to identify with the youth in my Church. The teenagers thought it was cool because I could speak their language and I knew their music and culture. The pre-teens appreciated the fact that I still knew how to have fun. Over the course of seventeen years, I baptized scores and scores of young people and I made it my business to follow them in school, in community and in life. I felt it to be my pastoral responsibility and Christian duty to be a role model for them. But, on a wholly personal level, I felt the need to repay the debt that I owed the deacons of my youth. I wanted to be there for the youth of my pastorate as those men had been there for me. I was determined to model what was best about living life for Christ as it had been shown to me in the faces and actions of the deacons of Mars Hill Church.

When I became Moderator of Cedar Grove Missionary Baptist Association, one of my personal priorities was to become a friend to young pastors and young preachers. I made it my business to invite every newly licensed preacher in the area to our Church to preach after their initial sermon. I gave them books, helped them develop sermons, and was brutally honest about their sermons. In retrospect, I suspect that I was much too hard on most of them and probably did more to discourage them in ministry than to encourage them. I always believed that the young preacher has far too many cheerleaders and far too few coaches. The role of the cheerleader is to make you feel better; the role of a coach is to make you play the game better.

As preaching coach to young pastors, I spent my own money to help buy pulpit robes, books and pay tuition. When they made the almost inevitable mistakes in pastoring their Churches, I did the behind the scenes work to patch the breaches that their indiscretions had caused. Some of them lacked a good relationship with the pastor who licensed them and I willingly filled that void for them just as a similar void had been filled for me. There were dozens of young men who fell under my guidance to varying degrees. Unfortunately, these were the days when Churches were not welcoming to women who were called to preach. It was sadly never my privilege to have a daughter in ministry.

In my final pastorate at Temple Memorial Baptist Church in High Point, North Carolina, I took a special interest in young adult men who had families. Many of these young men had come to adulthood on a trial-and-error approach to manhood. I spent a lot of time cultivating their trust and helping them compensate for their absent fathers or poor role models as a youth. It would not be fair to say that I was their mentor. Again, I was more like their coach. I stood on the sidelines of their lives, ready to offer the best plays and to be there for them when they needed to huddle and re-group. Many of these men had been baptized when they were young and joined the Church in their youth, but these experiences had been pro forma. It was important for me that I helped to guide them into a relationship with Christ. I encouraged them to read and internalize the Old Testament book of Proverbs. They all always seemed to have found some little nugget to encourage and inspire them. I remember often asking them if they'd read any good proverbs lately. Inevitably, they would quote one and start recanting how they were trying to live up to that and make it less than a mere mantra, but a model for living.

My role as Executive Secretary-Treasurer of our denomination in North Carolina does not afford me the opportunity to become very involved in the lives of individuals as I did when I was a pastor or moderator. This is the thing I miss most about having retired from the pastoral ministry. I do, however, continue to have a mentoring role as the Convention employs a number of young people as student interns who work in our building. The times have certainly changed and the prevailing themes of young adulthood are markedly different from what they were almost forty years ago when I started my pastoral ministry. But it remains true that many college aged young people have not benefited from the guidance of an African-American role model – especially a role model who is a Christian. I have felt it my duty to help bridge that gap as a core part of what ministry is in a denominational office.

Young pastors continue to find their way into my world even though I no longer serve in a pastoral position. Some of these pastors have told me that I have a "welcoming spirit" (whatever that is). I tend to think it is more because I tell really funny stories. It's not hard to become familiar with a person with whom you can laugh. So these young preachers huddle around me from time to time to laugh and joke and have a moment of release from the burdens of being a pastor-servant-leader. But, like Nicodemus, they sometimes come to me privately to unburden themselves and to tell me things that they vowed never to tell anyone else. Rarely do I have the answers, but there is healing in my willingness to listen. There is usually some vignette from my own ministry that I can share as a small bandage on what are sometimes mighty wounds. Rarely do they leave my presence with the answers they may have initially sought, but they always leave me with a sense that they have a friend and a listening ear should they need it.

I believe that we all amass a great debt across the years as others help to build our lives and contribute to what will become our station in life. We pay on that debt by giving back – in like measure – to other people who need our help and hope. Any minister who sees ministry only in the context of a preaching ministry has not fully grasped what it is to be in ministry. The New Testament records much of what Jesus said, but it gives us many more pictures of what Jesus did. If we are to model Christ, we have to be able to reference the points of contact that we make with others that betters their lives and brings them into deeper relationship with Christ. That will often happen as a result of our preaching, but it may more often happen as a result of our giving guidance, offering help, and displaying the best of our character. For me, I have spent all of my adult years being mentor, friend, big brother and sometimes dad to countless young, African-American men who have been in or near my ministry. Having done that work for so many years, I still believe that I have scarcely paid on the debt I owe to the men of the Church who were there for me in my youth. I suspect that I will never pay that debt in full.

The Chairman of the Board of Deacons in the Church of my youth and conversion was named Ulysses Boone. Deacon Boone was the head deacon of our little church and quite well respected in our community. He was, in many ways, a simple man. A farmer who provided for his family by the sweat of his brow. I do not know the extent of his education, but I would venture to think that he had no more than an elementary education at best. Deacon Boone inspired respect from the adults in our community and a sense of awe among the children. I am not certain that any of us understood why he was such a giant among men, but we just knew that he was. None of us children would ever want to disappoint him in any way.

Perhaps it is my own inflated remembrance, but the elders of the days of my youth were spiritual giants. You heard the strength of their faith in their songs. Their prayers exuded confidence in God and a certainty that better days were surely to come. If I close my eyes and concentrate, I can almost hear the prayers of Deacon Boone: *"This morning, our Heavenly Father, a few of your handmade servants come knee bowed and body bent before the throne of mercy. We have come to return unto Thee some well-deserved thanks for last night's sleep and this morning's early rising. We thank Thee, O Heavenly Father, that last's night's bed was not our cooling board and last night's sheets were not our winding sheets. But right early this morning, You touched these old feeble frames with a finger of Thy divine love and our eyes came open and we saw the brightness of a brand new day . . .* "Without fail, the entire Church would unite in some strange bond that rose and fell with the cadence of the Deacon's voice. Before long, a virtual symphony of word and pause, moan and joy, petition and thanksgiving would break forth like a rushing, mighty wind and literally fill the whole house. Such a spiritual man as this deserved our respect.

Our Church held "preaching service" only once a month on the third Sundays. There was a break between Sunday school and preaching service. Inevitably, as soon as the Sunday school was over, my friends and I would scamper out of the sanctuary and head to a clearing in the grass near the edge of the woods. Amid the green grass was a nearly perfect circle of dirt. Upon reaching that space, all of us would reach into our pockets. Out would come marbles from one pocket and penny candy from the other. There, careful to keep our knees on the grass outside the circle so as not to get our Sunday pants too dirty, we would shoot marbles in our free time before Church.

There was a grand cast iron bell in the steeple of that wood framed country church and it would ring minutes before the preaching service would start. For the longest time, my friends and I thought that God was somehow intervening in the affairs of eight and nine year olds to keep us from being late for service and, thereby, deserving the wrath of our parents and guardians. Upon hearing the first rich tone of that old bell, we would quickly gather what marbles we could and stuff them back into our pockets and run for the Church leaving a mess of penny candy wrappers in our wake.

It was not that we were that excited about worship. Quite the contrary! The aim of our scurrying in from the edge of the woods was that we might claim the last pew in the Church. We had convinced ourselves that if we sat on this pew we would be beyond the gaze of parents who sat up front or in the choir loft. We were too uniformed to realize that ushers and other adults closer to the back of the Church were perfectly positioned to spy on us and they would promptly report our indiscretions to our parents. For the longest time, we thought our elders could somehow see from the backs of their heads as we were punished for bad behavior in Church.

On this particular Sunday, there was a group of older women who were making their way to the front doors of the Church. There were only a few steps from the ground to the outer doors of the vestibule. My group of friends ran past these ladies and bounded up the three or four steps to the outer door. We were so close to that last pew of our heart's desire.

I was last in the group and just before my feet crossed the plane that was the outer door, I felt something catch me in the collar of my Sunday shirt. It was as if it lifted my small person off the ground. I turned to see that it was Deacon Boone. I think that Deacon Boone was the tallest person I knew. After having accosted me, he bent his face to mine. It was as if the clouds had come down to touch the ground. With a stern face and a very harsh expression, Deacon Boone said to me, "Boy, don't ever let me catch you running past women folk trying to get in the Church. You stand here like a little man and hold the door for them." There I stood: red faced, embarrassed, scared that my poor behavior would be reported to my grandmother, and dreading the ridicule I would have to take from my friends. I wanted to cry, but I was too embarrassed and only allowed a few sniffles.

It is amazing how scenes from years past become indelibly etched into our minds. Nearly half a century has intervened between then and now, but I remember it like it was yesterday. But somewhere in the economy of God, it was known that I would one day have to come up with a good definition of what ministry is. To me, ministry is holding the door open for someone else. That simple act of respect for others and loving others more than self is really what I have found ministry to be about. The person who holds the door for others may risk losing their preferred place. The door holder will surely lose something by serving others when one's needs and wants could easily be met by simply going in before those that we pass in life. Real ministry – like the example of Christ – means holding the door open for others.

There is something else that stays in my mind about that day. I don't recall even one of those women for whom I held the door thanking me. No word of thanks. No nod of appreciation. No smile sent my way. Not even a pat on the head. Likewise, the work of ministry will often be unappreciated. Most pastors will be feted once a year on the obligatory pastoral anniversary observance. Most pastors will occasionally be thanked for the work that they do, but they will more often be criticized for the work they leave undone. Ministry is sometimes a very thankless task. Sometimes this is the case because those to whom we minister are so self-absorbed or overwhelmed by their own personal circumstances. At other times, the attitude of those we serve boils down to a feeling that "that's your job." Far too often it is the result of this modern "me, myself and I" culture where the most important thing is always what I want and what I need. This can be discouraging. Over the many years that I have been in ministry, I have seldom been appreciated or thanked or recognized for many of the personal sacrifices that I have had to make to benefit others. Some times that has been due to my own reluctance to be praised or honored. At other times, it has specifically been due to the callousness and indifference of those to whom I have ministered.

I completed the task that Deacon Boone gave me that Sunday. After the last lady had come through, I closed the outer door and braced myself for the taunts I knew I would get from my buddies. I scarcely raised my head. But as I left the outer door of the vestibule and approached the inner door that led in to the sanctuary, I was surprised to look up and see the face of Deacon Boone again. It was not at all stern this time, but it was wonderfully decorated with a broad smile. His teeth were not perfectly straight, no doubt from poor to no dental care over the years and they were slightly tinged from the years of dipping tobacco which was normative for our community. The deep furrows that time had plowed into his forehead seemed to have vanished for a moment. His skin of his face, darkened by long years in the hot Virginia sun, seems to glow. His dark brown eyes that often seemed to sing a sad song of sorrow now seemed to have a twinkle. Even before he said it, his face showed his pride in me and his pleasure in my having completed the assignment given. As my feet came to the threshold of the inner door leading into the sanctuary, he patted me on the head and said, "That's a good boy." As I had held open the outer door for the elder women, he now held the inner door of the sanctuary open for me.

If I can be faithful at ministry and if I can keep the vows that I have made with God and if I can serve without reservation, one day I can expect that the One Who caught me in my collar and gave me His assignment will hold the door open for me. The sky will split, the clouds will part, the atmosphere will break and the Lord shall descend.

The dead in Christ will rise and those who remain will be caught up. When the saints go marching in through the doors to eternity which our Lord will have opened for us, hearing the welcome voice of Jesus saying "well done" will more than compensate for every tear and every fear, every perceived snub and every unacknowledged act of service. For that possibility, I am happy to hold the door open for others.

Lessons for Ministry

1. The Koheleth was right: *There is nothing new under the sun.* Our ministry is nothing more than the quilt work of persons who have influenced us and touched our hearts and spirits. A little bit of her, a little bit of him, a lot of this, less of that all come together to form the intricate patterns that is the quilt of our ministry. Accept and honor the influence of your elders who have given a swatch of some fabric to make you who you are. Be ever grateful for their influence.

2. Major in minor things and be attuned to the simple things in life. We are much too often about the pursuit of the profound, the never-before-heard, the unique and uncommon. But God very often gets our full attention through the simplest of things: the bright laughter of a child, the sorrow of a tear stained cheek, or the firm grip of a hand.

3. We begin ministry seriously in debt – indebted to the women and men of faith who invested in us and poured a bit of themselves into us. Without fail, none of these people who came in and out of my life ever wanted anything from me in return. Their pure motive was to partner with God to help make something meaningful out of my life. The only way I have known to pay down that debt was to help others as I was helped. We all have an obligation to "pay it forward."

CHAPTER 3

"YOU CAN'T MAKE ME DOUBT HIM, I KNOW TOO MUCH ABOUT HIM"

I F THE MEN in our Church taught me manhood, it was Sunday school that taught me about Christ. Even though our Church met for worship only once a month, we had Sunday school each week. I looked forward to Sunday school. Learning had always excited me and I found reading and writing to come easily to me.

I always received good grades in public school (except maybe "deportment" which was the grade given to how well a student behaved). It was fairly easy for me to figure school out: teachers would tell you something, you remembered what she said, and you wrote down what she had said when you were tested. In my young mind, it was not that hard. Because I had a good memory, the process was simple ... and boring. To compensate, I read a lot and was always interested in what the next chapter of our assigned reading might say. There were few books in our home as a child. There, of course, was the obligatory family Bible that lay centered on the coffee table in the living room, but no one ever read it and it was, I thought, the unpardonable sin to actually touch it. The occasional *Ebony* or *Jet* magazine found its way to our home, but that was never more than a few days reading. Fortunately for me, my grandmother had bought a set of *World Book Encyclopedia* and the accompanying *ChildBook* series. From about age seven or eight until age eighteen, I found some reason to turn to that library of facts and pictures. As I grew older, I used the encyclopedia to understand the arcane words of the King James Version. I often had to look up places and people in the Sunday school lesson. In addition to being invaluable for my school work, I found the encyclopedia to be essential to my understanding of the faith.

I had the best Sunday school teachers in my youth. Usually the person assigned to the youth class was a public school teacher. In our Church, youth class was all the young people – elementary through teens. In retrospect, it took a heroic effort to teach so wide an age range, but somehow they did. They did it through a combination of professional skill which they carried from the public school classroom and the reservoir of respect that public school teachers had in their communities. We would hardly challenge or disrespect the Sunday school teacher any more than we would challenge or disrespect the public school teacher. The fact was that they were one in the same. Either as reward or punishment (I never figured out which), I was often called upon to help the teacher by taking the younger ones a couple of pews away from the rest of us to tell them the Bible story that the lesson of the day referred.

The best part of the Sunday school experience for me was the opportunity to answer the teacher's questions or to ask questions. I enjoyed both. Both afforded me a chance to think about the lessons which were being taught and refine my understanding by asking or answering questions. While many of my friends peppered the teacher with questions to try to annoy her or best her, I always really wanted to know more about what the Bible was saying. I grew up in a culturally conservative environment where the elders were certain that there was a clear right and an even clearer wrong to everything. As a young person, I just accepted their answers. When I became a teenager, I was confounded at the difficulty of reconciling what the Sunday school teachers taught and what the real adults in my world did. Remember that my Sunday school morning was more likely than not preceded by a night at "The Store" when my young eyes and ears saw and heard almost everything that was in direct contradiction to what the Sunday school lessons taught. As a youth, I knew that I needed help reconciling the two worlds that I moved between.

I guess it was the combination of public school teachers and my Sunday school teachers drilling into my sometimes "poor in Deportment" head that education was the way out of poverty and into a better life. However, for some strange reasons, the preachers in my reach as a child and a youth never impressed upon me the need for an education in order to preach. There was this great disconnect between an education for life (which I thought essential) and an education for ministry (which I thought was optional.)

Here is a great surprise to many who have followed my ministry over the years. I never had a formal theological education. My first and only degree is a Bachelor of Arts degree with a double major in Social Work and English. I was licensed to preach two years before I left home for college, but it seemed impossible in my mind that I would make a living as a preacher so I chose Social Work. Our family had been the recipient of several government welfare programs when I was a child. From my perspective, the caseworkers who handled our case were never very kind or caring people. I thought I could do better so Social Work was the major that I declared. Since I had done well in English in High School, the decision for a double major came easily. If I didn't find a job as a caseworker somewhere, I could fall back on my English preparation and teach Beowulf at a high school somewhere. While I always felt that my destiny would be ministry, I had no appreciation for a theological education in my early years of ministry and no working concept of what it would mean to be in ministry full time. Much to my regret, when I came to a more enlightened understanding of what ministry required, it was never really convenient to find a path to seminary. Unlike others who made the requisite sacrifices to gain a graduate school education, I did not. I will regret that to my grave.

After finishing my four-year bachelor's degree in three years, I was a bit tired of school. Those who know that fact about my college days usually respond with praise for such an unusual accomplishment. They say I must have been terribly smart. I am not sure it was all about my being smart. It really had more to do with the fact that I could not afford four years of college. Those three years would initiate a pattern of hard work that would stay with me the rest of my career. I took eighteen to twenty-one credit hours each semester. I was in school for every summer school session taking two classes each term and one term tricking the dean to allow me to take three classes. While working and studying, I worked two work-study jobs: one in the college's theatre department and another in either the Registrar's office or the Office of the Dean of Academic Affairs. In addition to that, I picked up any odd jobs I could find. I did everything from painting buildings to teaching English to Vietnamese immigrants to helping lift corpses into caskets in the morgue of a local funeral home. And, of course, I was delighted to get a chance to preach a sermon at any church that would offer an honorarium.

It wasn't that I was greedy or enamored by money. I actually have never been. It was that I came from a poor background. I was fortunate to receive sufficient government assistance to pay for room and board at college, but all the other things that life requires had to be earned from the sweat of my brow. Our family had little resources to help me financially while I was in college. An explosion of joy and thanksgiving went off in my very soul the few times during my college career that a twenty-dollar bill came in a letter from my mother or my great grandmother. My several jobs during college provided the resources for me to live independently and also afforded me the chance to send money back home to my grandmother to help with the mortgage and the expenses of running a household in which I would never live again.

Immediately after my undergraduate degree, I was tired. I was called to my first congregation while still a senior in college. After graduating, I became busy in the lives of my parishioners and in the community where our church was. Later I started adopting teenagers and that busied me so that there was no time to think about furthering my education. Over time, ministry for me included public service, social justice advocacy and community activism. Graduate school was, in my mind, a thing to get to later. When I came to my second pastorate, I had already established the pattern of working long hours, trying to be ever available to members in crisis and helping to steer my adopted boys who were marching steadily into manhood through the high tides of young adulthood. I did not see a time for graduate school.

Though I never attended graduate school, most of my early ministry was full of grad school stuff. I cannot recall how many Master's theses or Doctoral projects that I proofread, punctuated and helped sentences make sense. Friends who were in seminary would meet at some awful hour post-midnight and talk about some class they were taking and I would debate and argue for hours over scrambled eggs and toast. I helped friends and acquaintances pay tuition and for books. Occasionally, a young scholar who had benefited from my financial support would convince his favorite professor to allow me to sit in on a class that he was taking. I was always around the edge of the seminary, but never stepped in. That was the biggest mistake of my ministry.

Because I did not have a formal theological education, I had to compensate (and some will say overcompensate) in other ways. I became an avid reader. When I retired from the pastorate after twenty-four years as a pastor, my personal library consisted of almost two thousand volumes. Most of them were read in total and, out of the others, I gleaned a chapter here and there. I hung around trained clergy and spent a lot of time listening. After a lively discussion about something, I would head to the local library the next day and attack the card catalog. Mind you, these were pre-Google days. Public television was an elixir when some program aired on religion or Christianity or history. I learned much from my friends who were seminary trained in discussions, debates and arguments about the Church, politics, the arts and the sciences.

I said earlier that I may have overcompensated for my lack of a theological education. I became ridiculously fastidious about appearing and being professional. I never sought to be a show off, but I have always felt some need to be accurate and correct and well-spoken as some kind of sin offering for my failure to have a graduate degree. My friends declare that I am the only human in creation whose texts messages are always grammatically correct and complete with punctuation and quotation marks when needed. In an age of e-mail, text messages and tweets, I still write letters. I labor for long periods over letters at times trying to be certain that my arguments are sound and my presentation as perfect as it can be. These behaviors stem from an ever present feeling that I missed much in choosing to sacrifice my own theological training because I was so wrapped up in the lives of other people, trying to make their lives better and their journey easier.

In 2006, Shaw University, the oldest historically black University in the south, conferred an honorary doctorate degree upon me. It may have been the most uncomfortable day in my entire life. Not only was I completely aware that I should never have been so honored in an academic setting, I sat on the stage that day next to the legendary Reverend Dr. Gardner C. Taylor who was similarly receiving an honorary degree that day. The late Dr. Taylor had preached around the world, been noted as the Dean of America's black preachers, and had been honored by Presidents of the United States. A long and distinguished career in preaching, social justice and pastoring New York's famed Concord Baptist Church of Christ distinguished Dr. Taylor from most and especially from me. Yet there I was on stage to receive the same high honor that was to be bestowed on him. My stomach was queasy during the entire ceremony – partly from the sheer gravity of the honor and partly because of this overwhelming sense of inadequacy. Nearly a decade later, I still shudder to think how unworthy I was of such a distinguished honor.

I have been called upon from time to time to speak or lecture on a college campus. I have politely refused them all. There is a mixed sense of shame that I never went to seminary coupled with a profound sense of inadequacy and feeling very much "out of my league." I have preached on University campuses over the years, but I have come to those moments confident in my gift as a preacher and never pretending to be an academic.

Most of the people with whom I interact on a daily basis address me as "Doctor." I am ever grateful for how they honor me with so lofty a title. However, a tiny piece of my self-esteem melts each time I hear it. I am the least worthy of all.

I actually prefer the title "Reverend." "Reverend" is the only title I have ever held in life that I had to constantly work to maintain. I am called "Mister" simply because of the doings of genetics and gender. I was called "Pastor" simply because I had a church and another clergy around me did not. I have been called "Moderator" which was the simple result of an election. My lack of a graduate school education makes me feel quite unworthy with the title "Doctor." I am called that only as an honor; I did nothing to earn it. I never took on the Biblical titles of "Bishop" or "Apostle" or "Elder." Under any of those titles, I would be too often reminded of Paul's advice: *"Do not think more highly of yourself than you ought."*

"Reverend" is the only title that has been given to me that I have had to work hard to maintain. The title is no self-aggrandizement of the holder of the title. It is a frequent reminder that I have an obligation to live up to my calling. "Reverend" says there is something holy, sacred and honorable about the work I am called to do. "Reverend" says there is more I have to do each day to be worthy of the respect of those who respect me, to be worthy of the trust those that follow my leadership have placed in me, and to be worthy of the work that God has given to my hand and heart and feet. I do not suggest that I have not, by word or action, sometimes sullied this title. I know that I have fallen far short of what it means and what it ought to be. But not one day has gone by when I have not reached into my best self to try to be worthy of that title. On that never ending task, I will labor until I die.

Whether in Sunday School or public school, in supporting others in their educational pursuits or in my compensating for my own lack of a formal theological education, my principal goal in life seems to have been etched on my heart: I have always chased the peace and calm, the strength and boldness that I had heard in the prayers and testimonies of the elders of our Church on the night of my conversion. I remember their voices rising to crescendo without the aid of piano or organ, drums or tambourine. With only hands calloused from work in the fields or from scrubbing the floors of other people's houses and feet weary from the long days of toil and labor that they endured without end in sight, they created a symphony in a barren land. Through raised windows that both let in the summer heat and let out that sometimes joyful, sometimes mournful refrain, it was as if all creation could hear them sing: *"you can't make me doubt Him, I know too much about Him."*

As a child, I knew that Sunday school would be a part of the journey to that place where I would not doubt Him and know Him. As a young adult, I thought a college degree would bring me closer to that end. In the morning of my ministry, I was convinced that reading and learning and listening would enlighten my path to a scoreboard that read "doubt 0 and knowledge 10."

As I reasoned it, the more I learned, the more likely I would come to know what their secret was. I wanted to feel again and again what I had felt on that third Thursday night in August. I wanted the holy boldness I had detected in my elders which made their voices rise and shake the rafters. I wanted to have whatever it was that squared their shoulders and brought tears to their eyes. However, as a child, it had so far eluded me. But I would pursue it relentlessly.

I would experience something like it again six years later, but this time it would be on a Tuesday night. The first time it inspired me; the second time it frightened me.

Lessons for Ministry

1. A formal theological education is essential in modern ministry. I neither recommend nor do I endorse the path that I took in this modern era. I am convinced that theological education helps the student to learn how to think and about what the student should think. Being able to think, clearly and deeply, is essential to success in ministry.

2. Realize and recognize your limitations. No one comes to ministry with a perfect score in every area of service. Some of us are better at this than at that. Recognize that. Work to improve yourself where you are weak, but also know that you will always have strengths and weaknesses. It may take a brutally honest friend or family member to help you see where you are weak. Pray that God will send someone in your circle who knows how to speak "truth in love."

CHAPTER 4

"I HEARD THE VOICE OF JESUS SAY"

I SUSPECT THAT THERE is not much more that a fifteen-year-old boy would prefer not to do than to be at Junior Choir rehearsal, but there I was. As a teenager, I was trusted to be at home more and my time at "The Store" had practically ended. I could find a lot of things to do on a Tuesday night other than to be dragged to a choir loft filled with fidgety children and teenagers way too cool for this. But those were the days where youth rarely challenged their elders and, if the rule was to go, you went – in body, if not in spirit.

Our Junior Choir had a "choirmaster." I supposed that his wife was actually choir director and he was primarily there to serve as the man to pick up and let off the children. It was interesting that both of them were members of another Church, but they faithfully worked with (and often in spite of) the youth who collectively formed the Mars Hill Junior Choir.

The Junior Choir was quite popular in our Church, but all adults think children who do anything in Church are adorable. I was never a person of any musical gift. I did not sing nor did I play an instrument. About the closest thing I did to playing music was skillfully balancing a quarter on the needle and arm of the family phonograph to hear the scratchy

45's that were in abundance in our house. As for taking any professional music lessons, it was out of the question. We had no money for that and we had no car. Even with that limited musical ability, I was given the lead in a song that became a hit with the Junior Choir. The song title was "Oh Mother, Don't You Worry About Me." A line in the refrain said, "God's got His arms wrapped all around me, Oh mother, don't you worry about me." Since we were only five days from the first Sunday when the Junior Choir sang, I knew we would sing that song nearly to death in rehearsal. It would be to the delight of our choir director and choirmaster, but to the highest irritation of my friends. "Try to get it right the first time so we can go home," the teenagers said to me.

Choir rehearsal always opened with some youth reading (or reciting a scripture passage) and some youth being drafted to pray. Looking back at it now, I suspect it was good preparation to keep us children from being shy public speakers. The adults teaching music would require that we stand straight, pronounce every word correctly, and speak loudly even though there was not one solitary soul in the audience on rehearsal night.

It was the Tuesday night before the first Sunday of February in 1976. The scene unfolded just as I have described with one twist. At prayer time, the Choirmaster called on me to pray. While being called upon to perform some function or another in worship was not uncommon, it was strange to be called upon without having been given prior warning. If nothing else, we would be told who would pray after scripture. With baited breath, we would wait to see to whom the task of praying would fall. Scripture was the easier part: it was either simply reading something from the ragged Bibles that were scattered in the choir loft or it was reciting the verse we had learned last month when the children were called up front to "give a Bible verse." If all else failed, the verse that says "Jesus wept" got us young people out of many otherwise embarrassing situations.

I didn't have a clue what I might say in my prayer and the young person called upon to read scripture was too brief for me to put a plan in place. As I stood to my feet, I guessed I would either begin with or end with the Lord's Prayer. All I was really focused on was getting through this choir rehearsal, going home to play records or watch TV and plait my hair really tight so my "fro" would be just right in the morning. I do not remember a word I said. I have no clue how long I prayed. But when I was done, every eye in the room was staring at me.

I have always desired to have some extraordinary encounter with God at those places where my will intersected with the will of the Divine. I was jealous of Moses for his bush that burned, but never burned up. I was envious of Daniel's sleepover with hungry lions. I desired that the sky would break and doves would occasionally descend for me. The truth of the matter is that I have never really had any experience with God that was so dramatic and of Biblical proportion. Although I have listened carefully to both the saints and the "ain'ts" speak of these wondrous and sometimes fantastical God-meets-humanity experiences, I have never had anything to share when they shared their experience. Such has eluded me.

While it is difficult to fully explain, my God encounters have tended to be very calming times for me. They seem to have happened in the quiet of my soul while the noise of life was being completely shut out by the Presence of the Divine. It has been as if, for a moment, I become both deaf and blind – hearing only a "still, small voice" and seeing an unseen path or direction or purpose. I have known that these times were of God primarily because, when they conclude, I am as resolute about what I am to do as I am about any other thing in life. I am as convinced of what God wants and requires as I am convinced that I need air and water to live or as I am convinced that only light chases the darkness away. What is faith to me – the substance of hope and evidence of the unseen -- becomes as unshakable as any other fact of life in those encounters.

I wish I could say that I have these times often, but that would be far from the truth. They have been few and far between. Perhaps their scarcity validates their importance. I really do not know. I have come to know God's purpose through people that God has sent into my life. I have come to know His will as epiphanies come to me as I read Scripture. I have come to know God's plans through the disciplines of fasting, prayer and worship. And I have also found my peace and place in His calling.

Perhaps the most nebulous thing in ministry is one's calling. It is like a fidgety toddler who squirms away from a mother trying to tie a shoe. It is as undefined as the crayons of a young child that pays no respect to the lines. It is as loud as the roar of the motorcycle engine that pierces the darkness of a summer's night. We pursue it all of our lives in order to put on it clothes that will help others define what it is. Yet defining it and clothing it is as elusive a task as finding the proverbial needle in a haystack. Though it hangs around our lives as a thick fog – everywhere present, it never allows us to contain it as one would fill a bucket from a stream. We reach out to grab it, to control it, to contain it, to explain it and it slips through our fingers as does sand on a beach.

And yet there is nothing more true, more real, more definite and more absolute than is God's calling to those who have embraced Him and it. One of my favorite questions to pose to young people in ministry when I meet them is "tell me about your calling to ministry." I delight in their struggle to get the words exactly right and how even the best-spoken of them tend to stumble and stammer. It is the elusiveness of trying to box one's call comfortably in some predetermined boundary that makes it real: real to them and real to those who have had like experience. I have now spent nearly four decades refining and defining, editing and adding to what I know as my call to ministry. The more chameleon-like my words and understandings are, the surer I am that it was of God.

I knew that something was wrong when I took my seat on the back row of the choir stand. Not only were all eyes on me, I could not remember anything I had done or said. There was only this sense of calm and peace that came over me. Two things were clear to me: first, there was something that God wanted me to do and, second, He had once again laid claim to my life. I did not struggle. I had no questions. I was not afraid. I was as sure of this as I was sure that the fast beating in my chest was of a heart touched by God.

I was totally distracted the rest of the evening. I remember nothing at all. It was as if time paused for me so as to allow me to collect all that had happened. The ride home with the choirmaster was more quiet than normal. He knew something was wrong with me, but had no clue. Maybe he thought it was the moodiness or rebelling of a teenager. Actually, I was struggling with the decision whether to tell anyone. In the ride from Church to home, I had resolved that the best thing for me was to ignore it, tell no one and, if God was serious, He would do it again. I could give Him my answer on the second time around.

I did not invite the choir master in our home, but I thanked him for the ride and bounded up the eight cinderblock steps into the back door of our house. The back door opened into our dining area which was crammed tight with a refrigerator, various plant stands, a china cabinet and a table with four seats. Somehow my knees weakened as I crossed the threshold of the door of our house. Unsteady on my feet, I made it to the first seat I came to at the table. I claimed that seat as the only available refuge I could find. Then I broke into uncontrollable tears. It was loud. It was near hysteria. I could not stop the river of water that was streaming down my teenage face.

Of course, this alarmed my grandmother who kept asking me what was wrong. The crying was so uncontrolled that I could not really speak. I would get a word or two out between the sobs, but she could make sense of nothing. She was alarmed, as well, because I had suffered with asthma as a child. She did not know if I was having an asthma attack or not.

Our immediate neighbor was Jesse Lee Sturdifen, one of the deacons in our Church who had mentored me as a child. It was this deacon that my grandmother called that night. Partly because we always called our deacons when trouble came and partly because the Sturdifens had vehicles and they might be needed to transport me the seventeen miles to the nearest hospital. Deacon Sturdifen came immediately, but it seemed an eternity. He found me still sitting at the table, crying without end.

The best that our deacon and my grandmother could figure out from my broken sentence was "The Lord wants … ." After much coaching, rubbing of my back and holding my hand, I was finally able to complete the sentence I had been trying to get out all night. "The Lord wants me to preach." The annunciation came as quite a shock to them both. I am not from an especially religious family. Though we believed in God and attended Church on a fairly regular basis, card parties and Motown and "Sunday School words" (the kind that were never actually used in Sunday school) were always a staple of life at our house. In those days, none of those were considered the "Christian" things to do. I never remember any family prayers and, other than the repetition of the standard grace before meals, there actually wasn't that much prayer going on in our house. I did not come from a line of preachers. As far as I know, I was the only one of my bloodline to make that audacious claim. All things considered, I could certainly understand why people would be shocked.

I eventually stopped crying so that I could make my statement clear. I was resolute about the fact that God had called me to do something and I knew it was to preach. I had not a clue about how to preach, when to preach, where to preach nor what to preach. I only knew that I had to preach and I would. Deacon Sturdifen called our pastor who lived away from our community. I never spoke with him that night, but was content to allow the Deacon to press the claim on my behalf. At the end of the conversation, the Deacon reported to me and to my grandmother that Reverend P. D. Hill, our pastor, wanted to talk to me on Sunday and, if I convinced him, he would set up something called a "trial sermon." I heard the words, but I had no clue what it meant. I only knew that there was something that God required of me.

Deacon Sturdifen was a Godsend in the weeks between my announcing my call to ministry and my actual first (or "trial") sermon. Although he and his wife had always taken an interest in me, he was vigilant in keeping up with me and knowing how I was doing. Some weeks after that night of tears, Deacon Sturdifen asked me why I cried so much that night. He feared it was symptomatic of my doubting the call of God. However, it was nothing like that. It was not doubt; it was not fear; it was not joy. It was the only way I could relieve myself of the great disappointment that I had in myself. In some sense, I was literally trying to wash my own failure away.

Six years ago when I had had that first encounter with God and joined the Church, I said "yes" to the questions our minister had asked me at the altar that third Thursday night in August. On the ride home from Church that Tuesday night before the first Sunday in February six years later, it had occurred to me that I had, this time, failed to say "yes."

By the time I was fifteen, it had become my custom to send off a one or two-line prayer after I got in bed. That night, I returned to the practice of my childhood and bowed my knees to kneel before the roll top writing desk that stood almost as a sentinel in my bedroom. The desk had become the closest thing I had out of which I could have a makeshift altar. I do not know what else I said in my first prayer after being called to preach, but I do remember two things I said: one was "yes" and the other was a vow to never hesitate in saying "yes" to God again.

Lessons for Ministry

1. The call of God is a wonderfully strange thing that is strangely wonderful. I suspect that the place where God and humanity meet and kiss will always be both wonderful and strange. Though we might never completely understand it, we can – thanks be to God – wholly embrace it. I know absolutely nothing about alternating versus direct electrical current, but I am confident that if I plug something into a socket in my house that the correct current is there to allow me to turn on a lamp. There is much that I am trying to understand about why God called me, but that in no way diminishes my certainty that He did indeed call me.

2. Look for the certain signs that God is reaching out to you. For me, it has most often been quiet and calming and the bringing of a sense of purpose. Whatever happens to you when you come to those places where humanity intersects with divinity, embrace that, pray for it, and do not doubt it.

3. Do not dismiss that the call of God may come in ordinary circumstances. We far too often expect it to come in bright shiny packages with neatly tied bows. Perhaps it does for some. But it is just as real when it comes plain and unremarkable. How it comes is much less important than the reality that it does come.

4. I have been called many times over the course of my ministry. None, however, has been as powerful as what happened to

me during choir practice on the Tuesday night before the first Sunday of February in 1976. I have at times been called to do and, at other times, my calling was don't. I have heard both go and stop, stay and leave, turn or retreat. What God has called me to do is much less important than the fact that He calls me and that I am resolute in my belief in Him and in my determination to be obedient.

CHAPTER 5

"WHEN I BECAME A MAN . . ."

B Y THE TIME Sunday rolled around and I had the chance to speak with my Pastor, the word had already gone forth. It appeared that everyone I encountered had heard about my being called to preach. I am so glad that it was real for if it had not been authentic, I would have had no retreat. In the minds of the people, it was a done deal. Long before I spoke with our pastor or a date for my "trial" sermon had been announced, everyone was marveling that Thelma Williams' grandson was going to preach.

I do not recall what my Pastor and I discussed when we met before Church to talk about what I had experienced. As far as I was concerned, it was a done deal too. Regrettably, it was not because of the certainty I had in my call experience, but I had been bolstered by the notoriety and hype that had overtaken our sleepy little community. At first, my teenage friends were not quite sure what to make of me. Soon, however, it became cool and a badge of honor to hang around me. Though I took every possible advantage to present myself as "holier than thou," they were excited about this new venture in which I was about to partake even if neither they nor I exactly understood it.

The celebrity in the community made me far too heady. Understand that persons being licensed to preach in those days and in our community was a rare occurrence. When it did happen, the person called (usually a middle aged man) would always declare that he had been running for years and years from his calling. I said "he" intentionally because a woman preaching in our community at that time was completely unheard of and would have been considered nothing less than scandalous. To be a fifteen-year-old with a credible call to ministry was unbelievable. My fame came too rapidly and spread too widely.

I was loving every minute of it. I had announced my call on the first Sunday of February and the date for my "trial" sermon would be the third Sunday of April. The date selected was not only our big "preaching" Sunday service, but it was also Easter. If our Church leaders thought this timing necessary to insure a large crowd, they were probably wrong. People would likely have come out at midnight to see the wonder of a boy preacher. I did very little to prepare myself for my first sermon in the eleven weeks separating my call from my preaching. Even less was done to prepare me for preaching. I met with our Pastor each Sunday before my first sermon, but only five Sundays separated one event from the other. Our real time together was only a few minutes after Sunday school and before the morning worship service. I had no ministers in our family to give me guidance or counsel. Our family did not really have that strong a relationship with other Churches so I could not turn to other pastors for help. Ashamedly, I admit that I spent much more time worrying about which of my friends would be there, what I would wear and did I have to have a haircut or could I do it in my "fro."

I wanted everybody to know and everybody responded in a positive and encouraging manner. Even my father's relatives – who had never really had very much to do with me or with my family – began to have some pride in the fact that I had my father's middle and last name. The respect, the fascination, the "way-to-go's" came rolling in like a high tide. I almost drowned in the accolades and praise. It came from friends as well as strangers. I was congratulated by church leaders and lay members. I had the attention of principals and all of my teachers. Well, that is except for one.

Eudora Welty Cooper was my high school business class teacher. She was one of my favorite teachers. She was a large woman -- in stature and in every other aspect of her personality. She was the Minister of Music at one of the Churches in the county and a very religious person. Apparently, she had never heard of the concept of the separation of Church and state. Every Monday, she peppered students in her business class as to whether they had gone to Church the previous day. If we thought we would get by with a simple naming of the Church where we had worshipped, our hopes would be dashed as she quizzed us about the sermon we heard or what choir sang or if we had made it to Sunday School. If that class lasted fifty minutes, Mrs. Cooper sometimes spent half of it in the Bible and not in our Business class textbook.

When the word of my call to preach was circulating, I was curious as to why Mrs. Cooper asked me nothing of it. She must have heard it. Nothing happened in Church life that did not eventually present itself at the oracle that was Eudora Welty Cooper. But she was strangely silent on my case. I simply thought that she was waiting for a formal announcement to be made by my Church. Then, I knew, she would embrace me, congratulate me and make all kinds of fuss over me. Her good student was going to be a preacher. According to the community grape vine, I was destined to be a barn burner. Surely, Mrs. Cooper would be a monument of support for me.

When she said nothing to me during the week leading up to the public announcement and open confirmation of my having been called, I just knew she would have plenty to say on the Monday after that Sunday's announcement. I bounded up the stairwell to the second floor classroom early. I was the first student to arrive. She had her normal "good-to-see-you" smile on, but she said not a word. She didn't even ask the proverbial "did you go to Church yesterday?" question. Nothing. Silence. Nary a word.

I was puzzled by this odd behavior, but I thought I had enough celebrants that I could soon mark Mrs. Cooper off my list of "preferred supporters." After a few weeks, however, I became a bit paranoid. Why is she the only person in all of creation who is not excited and beside herself because I am going to preach? Even more irritating was her indifference. When others brought up the subject, she changed the conversation or completely ignored the discussion. In near fear and panic, I had some friends agree to speak with Mrs. Cooper outside my presence and find out what she really thought. They did and they came away without a clue.

As the interim wait came to a close, I was completely without clue as to why Mrs. Cooper was being so mean to me. I took it very personally. Why couldn't she celebrate with me like all the world was? Why is she showing such sour grapes toward me? Why is the playfulness and banter all evaporated like the smoke from a candle flame? Would she seriously be as heartless as that toward one of her favorite students?

It seems that Easter Sunday came fast that year. The tradition of our Church was to hold a sunrise worship service with breakfast following. After that would be Sunday school and morning worship. My "trial" sermon had been set for 3:00 p.m. After seeing such large Easter crowds in two services that morning, my pride and ego (which had enlarged themselves like balloons with too much air) began to deflate a bit out of fear that my afternoon crowd would be significantly smaller. I had no reason to fear.

Our family went home to eat and dress. (We had saved our Easter Sunday best for the "trial" sermon and wore our "old" Church clothes earlier in the day.) Armed with a new suit of some indescribable shade

45

of green and my 'fro appropriately trimmed and tamed for the event, I was off to preach my first sermon. Since that night of uncontrollable crying, I had not been at all nervous. As a matter of fact, I was excited about the new world that was opening to me. I could not believe the number of cars that were parked everywhere at the Church when we arrived. A small crowd was lingering around the front entrance. I would later discover that they were waiting for ushers to bring chairs to put in the aisle. Our Pastor, Reverend Hill, was a stern man who rarely showed emotion, but even he was almost giddy at the turnout and the attention that his licensing a boy preacher had brought.

I was escorted into the pulpit and offered the center chair. As I looked out on the congregation, I saw friends, relatives and acquaintances of all stripes. In my heart of hearts, I knew I was the star of the show and I was loving every minute of it. However, as the service drew on, my euphoria began to dissipate like a leaky faucet. At first, the drip is an annoyance and ultimately it disturbs your sense of peace and it becomes the only thing that you hear. The realization of just how un-ready I was for this moment began to dawn on me and it terrified me. My forehead and my palms competed to see which would produce the most sweat. A nervous bouncing of my knee soon became uncontrollable. Instead of seeing the faces of supporters in the crowd, I began to see the faces of those who would judge me and my preaching. There was absolutely no guarantee that the great sermon I thought I would preach in my mind would actually come out of my mouth.

Two horrors came to me one after the other while waiting for my own Junior Choir to sing the song before my sermon. First was the image of Mrs. Cooper and the cascading questions as to why she had been so disinterested in my preaching. Maybe she knew something I did not know. She was a real Christian in every sense of the word and maybe she picked up on something or the other. Could it be that I was mistaken about my call and only Mrs. Cooper knew that?

Immediately after that moment of panic, a second and much more frightening thought came to mind: it had been almost two months since my experience in Junior Choir rehearsal and I had not felt nor had I experienced the presence of God like that since. I wasn't really sure if you were supposed to feel like that all of the time or not. I had not ever thought deeply enough on what I was going to do to have had the presence of mind to ask my pastor or my deacon or anyone. In actuality, I had spent the entire interim weeks enjoying the fame, soaking in the adulation, and relishing the great success that I would be. Moments away from standing to preach for the first time, I was in a panic.

The Junior Choir finished and various shouts of "amen" and "preach, son" rang through the crowded room. For a second, my legs would not follow the command of my brain. But in that moment of panic, fear and weakness, I ran to the place in my mind that would give me strength and courage. One more time, I was at Junior Choir rehearsal and, as I thought about what I had felt and experienced, I whispered to myself and to God: "Yes, Lord."

I wish I could remember more about the first sermon that I preached. It is all lost to history save the scripture text that I chose: *"When I was a child, I spake as a child, I understood as a child, I thought as a child, but when I became a man, I put away childish things."* That text is from Paul's letter to the Corinthian Christians, I Corinthians 13:11. I suspect that it was intended in some way to be my personal manifesto that I was now grown – a preacher, no doubt. I think I was trying to tell the whole world that I was very different from who I used to be. Honestly, I am not sure what it was nor what I was trying to do. No one had helped me with developing the sermon. No one had advised me on understanding the context from which I was preaching. No one had told me about being relevant to the people to whom you are speaking. I had always been a good student in English and the language arts. I relied on those strengths to write a good speech, I guess. I sincerely doubt that it was much of a sermon.

I am amazed that I can remember so much detail about that day now forty years removed. Yet I remember not one detail about the sermon save the scripture text. I don't know what it was titled. I don't know if I had any points. I can't remember if I told any stories. I can't even remember if it was pounded out on the manual typewriter that was kept under the bed in my room. It may have been written in longhand on notebook paper torn from a well-used English or science tablet. I do not recall if it was a full manuscript or an outline. It is all blank to me.

Whatever it was, it was a hit. When I was done, the accolades and praise that I had so enjoyed for the past two months came again like a flood. Those who had been generous before were simply way over the top now. I am sure that it was a combination of pride in me and awe at the feat I had accomplished. Whatever it was it was enough for the Mars Hill Baptist Church of Capron, Virginia to grant me a license to preach. More than anything I was relieved that it was over. But there was a sinking feeling that something had really gone wrong. It felt more like a task completed than an accomplishment achieved. Later that night, a kind of sad solemnness (or maybe it was a solemn sadness) came over me. The realization that came to me was this: I had done nothing to try to please God in that first sermon. I was only interested in living up to the high expectations that the people had placed on a very young kid. I felt that I met their expectations, but I also felt that I had failed God's. I wasn't exactly sure how I would do it, but I resolved never to let God down again. I would think more of Him and less of me. I would surrender all and that would include my vanity, my ego and my pride.

School did not meet on Monday as the public schools of the day were closed on Easter Monday. I went back to high school on Tuesday. I had left that building the prior week as merely one of hundreds of students.

I returned as the only preacher among them. I was more humble and more intimidated about my new life than I thought I would be. What I wanted more than anything was the routine and the familiar. I wanted to chart no new courses as the one I had just embarked upon looked much too big for me.

I went into the Business class of Mrs. Eudora Welty Cooper and she posed to me the perennial question: "Did you go to Church on Sunday?" We both broke into laughter as I knew she knew what had occurred on Sunday past. She proceeded to tell me that she had heard all about it and was quite proud of how well she had heard that I had done. She offered to do anything that she could to help me and would pray earnestly for me. Our conversation was cut short as other students came in the classroom and Mrs. Cooper felt it nothing less than her Christian duty to query them on where they had spent Easter Sunday.

When class was over, I stopped at Mrs. Cooper's desk before taking leave to my Science class which followed. I told her that I had a question and she told me to ask it. I asked her why she had been so indifferent to me when everyone was so excited about my call to preach. I was surprised to hear her say that she was as excited as everyone else when she had heard the good news about my preaching the Good News. I immediately pressed her on why she had been so silent with her feelings and she, in return, impressed something on my heart that has stayed with me throughout my entire ministry.

Mrs. Cooper said she had no doubt when she heard that God had called me to preach. In her mind, she always felt that it would happen sooner or later. I pressed her as to why she did not share her feelings. She told me that she really wanted to, but she understood that her opinion was very important to me. She went on to say, "If God had called you to preach, I wanted you to preach because you knew God had called you and not because I or anyone else thought that you should." That was the first of many very helpful but hard lessons I would learn in life and ministry.

It is so easy to do what we do because of the constantly growing expectations of the people we know and love and serve. It is not out of the ordinary to frame our ministry more on the expectations of those around us rather than on the One Who called us. While the influence of Christian people whom we love and whom we trust is invaluable to our journey in ministry, it must always be significantly less than our conviction that we are doing what God would have us do and traveling in the direction that God would have us go.

That time between the announcement of my call to preach and my first sermon was a very dangerous time for me. I have to admit that my foot almost slipped. I suspect that I got caught up in the aura of ministry and not in the practice of ministry. Of course, much of that is due to the fact that I was a teenager who was struggling to understand life as well as to understand ministry. I know that it had much to do with my lack of guidance as I prepared to preach. I am certain that a large part of it was foolish expectation that God would always come to me as He had done on the night of my call. It never occurred to me that it was as much my responsibility to seek after Him.

Eudora Welty Cooper taught me a lot by not teaching a thing at all. Her instruction has bided well with me across the years of my ministry. I am ever grateful for people like her who stepped on the path that I was traveling and, when needed, stepped in my way.

If this were not a true story, this would be the point where I would say that I made no more mistakes and I had no further failures. However, the next chapter in my ministry can only be described in the words of my grandchildren. It was a "hot mess."

Lessons for Ministry

1. Distractions are ever present in ministry. At times, the distraction may be the busy-ness of ministry. At others, it may be the inability to distinguish the major from the minor. At others, it may be an absence of the spiritual disciplines that keep the soul nourished and the spirit strong. Develop ways to stay focused and ways to test your focus.

2. The preacher in the African-American context stands on a pedestal. It may be a pedestal that the preacher has built or it may be a pedestal that the people have built for the preacher. However, it is rarely true that the thing that God builds for His preachers are pedestals. The preacher, more than anyone else, must practice humility. It is an intentional task to be like Christ -- meek and lowly. I am concerned that many modern clergy miss the mark on humility and service. Instead, many seek (and too often demand) prestige, power and prominence. While these are not in and of themselves bad, they are not meant to be stolen from the people we lead, but they are intended to be earned from the people we serve.

3. Every minister needs someone who will be brutally honest. Even though we are built up and encouraged by people who compliment us and who make us feel good about what service we are offering, we still need the people who love us enough to let us know that we are indeed "a hot mess." If one only hears about what one does well, that minister will not have opportunity to improve where weakness reigns. I do not believe that we should encourage criticism from everyone who has an opinion. There are those who delight in demeaning ministry and some criticize only for the sake of being a critic. Find someone who loves you enough to be honest with you. And then love them for loving you that much.

CHAPTER 6

"SOMEBODY PRAYED FOR ME
... HAD ME ON THEIR MIND"

F EW OF THE people who have followed my ministry know that the
Shady Grove Baptist Church of Pelham, North Carolina was not
really my first Church. I was only twenty years old when I became pastor
of Shady Grove and I continue to refer to that beloved congregation as
my first church. But three years earlier, at the tender age of seventeen, I
was called to my true first church. Sort of. Kind of. Maybe.

After my initial sermon, I continued to enjoy being the local religious
Phenom. I had been humbled by the experience of the "trial" sermon
and become much more somber about my calling. However, I was
critically both uninformed and misinformed. I knew little of what it
meant to be a minister or be in ministry. Unfortunately, the library
of a public high school had virtually nothing about ministry. When
I could catch a ride with someone who was bound for Courtland,
Virginia to shop at Mitchell's Grocery Store, I would be dropped off at
Walter Cecil Rawls Public Library, the sole public library in the county.
While my beneficent driver was shopping for local delicacies like Dan
Doodle sausage and cabbage or greens, I would be likewise scouring the
shelves of the public library to find something that would nourish my
preaching. Occasionally, I came across some very helpful materials, but

more often than not, I found myself in the history or literature stacks of the library.

I knew that I knew little, but that simply did not comport with how much I was in demand as a child preacher. I had the youth day sermon market in my bag. Youth revivals were coming into vogue and I would always get invitations to preach at least one night. I was often invited to preach on Sunday mornings at churches where the pastor just needed a vacation. I drew exceptional crowds. For many churches in our local community, it was a good thing to have the boy preacher on the program, whatever the program was.

My grandmother's best friend was a part time seamstress and Miss Gertrude was engaged to design and fabricate my very first clerical garment. The buying of a professionally made pulpit robe would come much later. Not only did I not have access to a place that sold pulpit robes, I had no money for something like that. Miss Gertrude agreed to undertake the official robing of the local boy preacher. Over the weeks that followed, we all learned that sewing a traditional Wesley pulpit robe from scratch was no easy task. After several weeks and too many indefatigable fittings, the project was reluctantly scaled back from a robe to a cape.

Using the brightest red polyester fabric apparently known to humanity, Miss Gertrude created a floor length red cape for me. It draped my puny shoulders and traveled my entire frame until it came to a stop about a half inch from my shoe heel. It had a fairly elaborate button and loop enclosure which held the front together and an eye and hook contraption that held it together at the neck. After my first couple of sermons in the cape, it was returned to Miss Gertrude's sewing room so as to add slits for my hands. Carrying a Bible and maneuvering in and out of pants pockets underneath a floor length red cape was a strange sight indeed. One of my high school buddies who regularly followed my preaching told me that the sight of me fidgeting with a Bible under that cape looked as if I was arm wrestling with squirrels in the pulpit. The piece de resistance of the garment was two white embroidered doves, one on each breast. I knew enough about the faith to know that descending doves were a symbol of the descending Holy Spirit. So I chose doves. I wish I had also known that Miss Gertrude was a seamstress and not an embroiderer. The descending doves did not look anything like each other or very much like birds at all. One fairly resembled a church fan and the other took on a more clamshell-like appearance.

But no matter. I was clearly aware that this was an act and a labor of love on the part of my grandmother and her seamstress best friend. I was proud to wear it. My grandmother was proud as well. She had very few ways to contribute to my budding ministry. She had only an elementary school education. We had no car that she could drive me from church to church. She had very little extra money to buy me the sorely needed "Church clothes" that I lacked. This cape, in retrospect, was her playing a major part in my preaching ministry. I have never forgotten that and I was forever grateful for the thoughtfulness behind the act. With so outlandish a preaching attire, my popularity only increased. In retrospect, I remember that everyone wanted to "see" me preach; I recall very few persons who were interested in "hearing" me preach.

Over time, I developed the requisite antics to match my clerical garb. Even to this day, I use my hands way too much when I speak, but usually the hands correlate with what I am saying. Back then, my hands were totally unpredictable and out of control. They might flail aimlessly through the air. I was known to clap loudly and unexpectedly for no practical reason at all. It was not uncommon for my outstretched hands to be turned into a fist. I never knew why. Perhaps it was nervous energy.

I took to coming out of the pulpit on a whim. Cordless microphones were unheard of and the microphone on the pulpit lectern was solidly attached thereto. Since some of the churches in which I preached had no artificial amplification, it was not uncommon for me to be very loud when I preached. So I would holler in the pulpit for a while and come out of the pulpit and holler some more in the aisle of the church in which I was speaking.

I suspect it would have been humanly impossible for an African-American teenager in the seventies with a cape not to mimic and slightly modify what James Brown did on stage. I had no Maceo upon whom I could call, but I could publicly disrobe (or, perhaps it is more accurate to say, de-cape) on a moment's notice. With great fanfare and flourish, I could use the cape as a distraction when I realized (at the last minute) that something in my sermon was incorrect or didn't make sense. The cape distraction helped me find time to move further into the pages of my manuscript to something that really made sense. It is very clear to me that I was not being insincere or playing with the call that God had placed on my life, but when I didn't quite know what I was supposed to do, I did the first thing that came to my mind.

After about a year in ministry and close to my seventeenth birthday, I was approached by the leaders of the Bryant's Baptist Church of Courtland, Virginia. Courtland and Capron were only about eight or nine miles apart and Bryant's had been on my high school bus route. I passed the church daily. I don't recall ever having worshipped there before, but I certainly knew something about the church. Bryant's had recently built a brand new church building under the leadership of the late Dr. J. W. Worrell. At that time, Dr. Worrell was advancing both in age and in poor health so the church leaders were interested in finding a younger minister to assist Dr. Worrell. They came to me with a proposal.

Their idea was to employ me as "Junior" Pastor or Assistant Pastor. (They used the terms interchangeably. I did not at all care about the adjective in their sentence construction, but I was delighted with the noun – pastor!) At present, they were worshipping one Sunday a month, but they were going to add another Sunday, second Sunday, as youth Sunday. I would primarily preach on the second Sunday. If Dr. Worrell were unable to attend Church on some fourth Sundays, I might be asked to preach then as well. The deal was sealed when I was offered a regular "salary" of $15.00 per Sunday. (Of course, I would only be paid if I preached. Attending church as "Junior" or "Assistant Pastor" did not count for salary if one was not preaching.) A deal was struck, an agreement was reached and I was a pastor, albeit either "Junior" or "Assistant." I really did not care which was more accurate.

That "call" was a validating experience for me. I knew that I had serious deficiencies as a preacher, but I was trying very hard to give it my best effort. My prayer life was rich. I read everything I could find that even vaguely spoke of faith. I listened attentively to other preachers preach and I mimicked much of what I saw and heard. Like the Ethiopian eunuch of Acts, I was reading books and watching preachers and studying the Bible and copying mostly everything I had seen done in pulpits, but I had no one to help me understand any of it. The simple fact that I had been "employed" by a church made me feel that I was on the right track. I recognized, as well, that I had a long way to go.

Just as there are two sides to every coin, I later came to realize that the leaders of Bryant's Church also had their plans for me. Dr. Worrell's age and infirmities were not at all contributing to church growth. Inasmuch as they had just completed a new building with a fairly large monthly mortgage payment, the leaders knew that they had to do something to fill the pews and, by extension, fill the Church's coffers. Since I would be certain to draw a crowd (and, with the crowds, money for the offering), it was a prudent business move to sign up the hottest thing around. They were getting a very good deal for $15.00 a sermon or $30.00 a month.

Within weeks after I was named to the Church staff of two people (Dr. Worrell and me), the good Doctor took critically ill. He never returned to the church. He lived in Petersburg, Virginia which was about a fifty-mile commute one way. At that distance, I would never have a chance to visit with him and consult with him about what needed to be done at the Church. Anyway, I was struggling to find transportation to get to Bryant's on preaching Sundays. Seeing that $5.00 of my $15.00 salary regularly went to pay whatever poor soul would pick me up and take me back home, I never would have had enough money to pay someone for regular trips to visit and receive instruction from Dr. Worrell. Even though, I had no access to the Senior Pastor which (under normal circumstances) would have been a problem, it was quite the delight for the Church leadership. It afforded them unfettered control of the affairs of the Church. They were lucky to have a Senior Pastor too sick to attend to affairs of the Church and a Junior Pastor too naïve to lead the Church.

While it was the perfect arrangement for the Church leadership, it was the perfect storm for me. I was never told exactly what Sundays I would preach. It was not uncommon for me to arrive (red cape and all) to find that someone else had been engaged as preacher for that Sunday. While a guest preacher preached, I would sit in the pulpit, not much more than living, breathing decoration for the benefit of the "real" preacher who had been invited to preach. I never attended a business meeting. The deacons told me I was not needed there. I never consulted with or attended a meeting of any Church auxiliary. (I did come to a Junior Choir rehearsal once. I thought I had been invited to motivate and inspire the young people. Instead they wanted me to sing with the Junior Choir on the Sundays that I did not preach. I politely declined.) I never had keys to the Church nor was I asked to have anything to say during worship except for my sermon. Eventually the Church stopped putting "Pastoral Briefs" on the morning worship service program and just extended the announcements time during which the Church Clerk spoke. I was, however, allowed to use the Pastor's Study for putting on and taking off my now famous red cape, but I was told to never sit at the Pastor's Desk.

I stayed at Bryant's until I left for college a little over a year after they had "called" me. As with anything new, sooner or later, the novelty wears off. After a few months, I preached less and less and, having satisfied themselves with having "seen" – not "heard" -- the boy preacher, the crowds moved on to the next new, shiny object. When I could not draw the crowds that came in large numbers to Bryant's, I became dispensable. Why spend fifteen whole dollars on him? I was never fired, but more and more of my Sunday mornings became suddenly free.

I have never believed that there was any malevolent intention on the part of the Church leaders. They had a real concern for the future of the Church now saddled with mortgage debt. I was simply a resource, as they saw it, to be used to raise money and increase the exposure of the Church to the larger community. Although it was, in almost every regard, a horrible experience for a new preacher, I do not believe that they intended that for me. It was the natural result of Christian people who sometimes forget what it is to be Christian. It was what always happens when Christians depend more on walking by sight and not by faith. I was complicit in my own demise as I used the best of my showmanship to give them what they wanted: a memorable experience that would make the people come back for more. It occurred to neither of us that authentic, meaningful worship would do that even better than did my showmanship.

One of the most influential members of the Bryant's Church was a school teacher named Mahala Williams. Mrs. Williams had never taught me, but she, like every other school teacher in the region, was highly regarded. As her husband was a deacon of the Church and involved in making the hard (and small) decisions for running the Church, I think she was acutely aware of how much I was feeling shut out. I said nothing to anyone, but a sense of melancholy began to engulf me whenever I went to Bryant's. I began to dread the Sundays that I was supposed to be there. Mrs. Williams seemed to sense my growing dissatisfaction.

Upon arrival one Sunday morning, Mrs. Williams came to the Pastor's Study – the door was always open as I was not allowed to ever close it. One deacon had told me that the adults always needed to know what might be going on behind that door. People walked in and out freely and without the courtesy of a knock or asking for permission to enter. So did Mrs. Williams on that particular Sunday. She asked me to go with her into the fellowship hall of the Church and to bring my Bible along with me. As I always did, I followed the instructions of adults although I had no idea what she wanted.

I arrived with Mrs. Williams to find thirteen other people already there. It was clear that the meeting – whatever it was – had been orchestrated by Mrs. Williams. Knowing that her husband was a deacon in the Church only raised my anxiety level even higher. All manner of possibilities swirled through my head. (The Bryant's Church was located just outside Courtland, Virginia. The original name for Courtland was Jerusalem. The whole time I was with the Church, I could not help but remember what they did to Jesus just outside Jerusalem.) I finally concluded that this would be the day of my crucifixion in some form or another. I was happy that they had decided to do the deed before worship began as opposed to making me wait for the certain death I convinced myself was surely on the way.

Mrs. Williams took the floor with a speech she had clearly been working on for a while. I don't recall her exact words, but it was designed to be a "pep" talk. She told me how the members of the Church all loved me and how they had great expectations for me. She remarked about how all of her colleagues that had ever taught me said I was a smart and able student. She encouraged me to continue my education after high school. The gist of the speech (as I took it then) was that I was a fine young person and maybe – one day – I might become a fine preacher as well.

She asked me to open my Bible and turn it to the last blank page. The Bible in question was the leather-bound New Scofield Reference Bible, King James Version. It had been presented to me on the Sunday of my "trial" sermon by the congregation that also gave me a preaching license. I never went anywhere to preach without it. It was a treasure and a constant friend. I opened the book to the last blank page beyond the concordance and maps. These appended items (along with Jesus's words in red) were the signature features of this particular and popular Bible. She took an ink pen from her purse and had each person in that room sign their name in my Bible:

Sarah S. Harris

Emma P. Boykins

Deborah S. Worrell

Mahala D. Williams

Della C. Williams

Margaret O. Worrell

Rosetta E. Robinson

Margaret Worrell

Vicki Worrell

Adell G. Ford

Lillie Mae Leigh

Ruben Mason

Wilbert Williams

Louis Barnes

When the signing ceremony was complete, Mrs. Williams told me that the fourteen people who had signed my Bible had agreed to regularly pray for me. She said they would pray for me while I was at Bryant's and when I was gone. She promised that I would have their prayers when I went off to college and throughout my young adulthood. She assured me that they would be praying for me by earnestly calling my name to the Lord whether they knew what I was doing with my life or not. I would always be with them in prayer.

That old Scofield Bible is still in my possession. After forty years, it shows the signs of age. Some pages slip out of place. The leather cover is worn and the color no longer uniform. The pages no longer adhere to the spine. It is no longer the mighty tool for ministry as it once was. It is now a treasured and fragile relic of a time long removed.

Every now and again, the demands of ministry and the stresses of life make me feel that sense of melancholy and dissatisfaction that first came to me many years ago while I "ministered" at Bryant's Baptist Church. In many of those times, I have been guided by an unseen Hand to the top shelf of the library in my home where my most prized possession is that Bible given to me so many years ago. In those lonely hours of discontent, I tend to open that tattered and battle-worn Book from the back cover and find that nearly sacred page. Time has faded the names that were once bold and clear. Some are barely readable. All of the signers have moved into houses not made with hands.

And yet this calm and reassurance floods my soul when my finger follows every line written on that page. I have no way to verify how long they kept the covenant that they made with me that day. I cannot even certify that they ever did, but I have felt throughout my life the certitude that someone who cared for me and who believed in God's call to ministry was praying for me. I believed that they were indeed speaking to God on my behalf and, in the language of those faithful souls of my youth, they were asking God to "strengthen me where I was weak and prop me up on every leaning and falling side."

Lessons for Ministry

1. If one truly believes that their path in ministry is being guided by God, that minister must also accept the fact that God is guiding them into pleasant and productive fields of service just as He guides one through the hard and stony places. There is something to be learned (and even earned) in the tough places for ministry. While all of us desire the higher places, God has every right to lead those who accept His call through both low places as well as high.

2. If God sends us to places that strain our patience and callous our hands in service, take courage in two things. First, it really is God's plan. Know that God's plan is large and expansive. Our ministry, whatever and wherever it is, is only one part of God's large plan. Accept the idea that my piece of the puzzle is necessary to complete the final picture that God wants to show us. Secondly, if God leads us into low and hard places of service, He will also send persons to minister and encourage us. They will fly into our lives like ravens roosting beside a dry river bringing us sustenance for our souls, nourishment for our spirit and strength to make it through. Who are these people, you ask? Don't worry. You will know them and they will know you.

CHAPTER 7

"I'M YOURS, LORD ...
TRY ME NOW AND SEE"

THE LAST CHAPTER pretty well closes my youth and earliest days in ministry. There are other stories that could be told, but none would be necessarily instructive. Hilarious maybe, but not terribly helpful in telling the story of my early ministry. As well, the untold stories of my days as a teen preacher would likely not inform others who are in the morning of their ministry. Principally, what I want to share has to do with the avenues of service that account for thirty-six of my forty years in ministry. For twenty-four years, I was a pastor: seventeen years in one parish and seven years in the second. For the last twelve years, I have been a denominational executive. These comprise the core of how I have served God and tried to be true to His call. But before I can tell the story of those years, there are some other quite critical influences on my life that deeply impacted my ministry. I fear that the accounts from my pastorates and denominational work may not make much sense if I do not also share what those influences were. This chapter and the three chapters that follow are my attempt to put those experiences, people and places into a certain context to help explain why I have become the person that I am.

If you have noticed a particular pattern of God using teachers to guide and instruct me, you are indeed right. I do so regret that I rarely recognized them as agents of God's help and God's plan in the time that they worked with me or worked on me. As I look back over the years, it is clear to me that God used these educators to move me into various positions that advanced my journey on life's often circuitous road. I do not know if any of them had a clue that they were being used by God in some magnificent, holy conspiracy to make me into whom God wanted me to be. I suspect that they did not. I suspect that they contributed to my life simply because to do so was what they were called to do. I am sure that my teachers helped hundreds of others. I suspect that I was no more important than countless young minds that were being shaped by their skillful methods. While each of them could have found professional satisfaction without ever having known me, I am convinced I never would have found professional achievement without my having known them. Before I can move on to share the other major influences in my life and to my ministry, there is one more teacher that you must know and one more story from my pre-college years that begs to be told.

Eva S. Pope was a very influential local educator. Mrs. Pope was my fifth grade reading teacher. While reading had been my good friend before coming into Mrs. Pope's fifth grade class, she made reading my lifelong companion. She was quite a regal woman, always as well-spoken as she was well-dressed. She had a commanding presence in the classroom. Her perfect diction and eloquent enunciation commanded the attention of her students and won the respect of her students' parents. She clearly enjoyed what she did and she did it extremely well. As impactful as my time in Mrs. Pope's class was, there were two interactions that made indelible impressions on me. The first impacted me quite negatively; the second helped me quite wonderfully. Eight years separated the two interactions.

One day when I was a student in Mrs. Pope's fifth grade reading class, she called me to the front of the class unexpectedly. I guess all boys are scared nearly to death when singled out by a teacher. I could not imagine what she could have wanted, but all manner of fanciful thoughts came to mind. Had I done something wrong? Had she found some note that I had passed to that little girl with the long hair that I had a crush on? Did she find out that I sometimes gave my free lunch ticket to a classmate who may have lost his lunch money? Whatever it was, I just knew it had to be bad.

When I stood beside her desk and turned to face the class as she had instructed, I knew that this had to be what a person facing a firing squad must feel. I had absolutely nothing of value to leave to anyone else, but I began to regret that I had no Last Will and Testament. At this point, I don't think I was as much scared as I was confounded. I had been a very good student and more respectful than most of my peers. I was absorbing the lessons much like a dry sponge drinks up water. I never failed to turn in assignments and I volunteered to do the weekly chalk eraser cleaning by beating the erasers against the bright red school building wall until the wall and my hair were white as snow.

Adding to my anxiety was the fact that Mrs. Pope and I lived in the same neighborhood. Neighborhood may be a strange way to describe proximity in the community in which I was raised. It might be better to simply say that we lived on the same road. Several miles on a rural Southside Virginia road did actually configure a neighborhood. She regularly drove past my house while en route to work or church or shopping. More important than that, Mrs. Pope's daughter actually lived just three houses away from mine. My point was, if Mrs. Pope had some reason to be displeased with me, she easily could have stopped by my house and shared her concerns with my grandmother. She did not have to make a public spectacle out of me in front of my peers.

Suddenly it occurred to me that I had never seen Mrs. Pope call up a student like this before. In the past, the call from the teacher's desk had been to write on the chalkboard or to take a note to another teacher or to pick up or return a book to her desk. To be asked up front and told to face the class must mean I had committed some egregious sin. In the mind of an eleven-year-old, the punishment had to be severe. The melody of an old prayer meeting song began to play in my mind: *"This may be, this may be, my Lord; this may be; may be my last time, I don't know."*

Much to my initial surprise, Mrs. Pope announced to the class that I was the first student who had ever made a perfect score on some or another reading test that she administered every school year. I cannot recall if it were some state-mandated standardized test or some instrument that she had concocted much like a mad scientist would have created in a secret laboratory. I was so irritated that she would call me out before the entire class for what was, in my mind, nothing remarkable at all. She kept emphasizing that perfect score of 100. Processing information as only a pre-teen can, the more she talked about what a grand achievement this was, the more I kept thinking that she must have had some really unintelligent students all these years if I was the only one to get a perfect score. To me, test taking was not really that hard. This was long before my own experiences as a school board member made me to know that good test taking skills are often a learned behavior. It is not natural for everyone.

Mrs. Pope went on way too long and was much too generous in her praise. I was feeling more and more uncomfortable about the entire ordeal. Why wouldn't she just leave it alone? Was I the only student whom she had planned to humiliate for the day? Exactly how many times could she say "perfect score" in one speech? I thought I saw contempt on the faces of some of my classmates. The handful of students that I did not get along with well in school just happened to also be in her class. I could see the anger and jealousy rise in their hearts and display on their faces. Only a couple of students (including the girl whose long hair had inspired me to write and pass notes in class) shared Mrs. Pope's joy at my accomplishment.

When the deed was finally done, I quickly returned to my seat, red face and all. I resolved that I would never go through anything like that again. Following Mrs. Pope's "praise-fest," I made a conscious effort to always get at least one answer wrong on Mrs. Pope's tests. I still made "A's", but I didn't ever want to be singled out for making "the perfect score" again. To add insult to the injury she had caused me, it was my aim to get back at Mrs. Pope by always giving the wrong answer to the easiest question on her tests. That always dumbfounded her. She would frown when returning a test paper to me and marvel at how I did not know the answer to this or that question. I always shrugged and said I would do better next time. However, it was a lie that I intended to do better the next time. It is only a fifth grade mind that would reason that I was getting back at her for the embarrassment she had caused for me by answering a question incorrectly.

Looking back, I am perfectly aware that Mrs. Pope had nothing but honorable and pure intentions. She wanted to congratulate me, to inspire other students, and to motivate me to continue to excel. I know that now, but I was much too tender in age and inexperienced in life to appreciate that fact then. Although very well intentioned, that experience has been omnipresent in the corners of my life. I cannot remember a time when I did not shun the spotlight and had been very uncomfortable to be the recipient of too much flowery congratulations. I simply do not like being feted and I do not accept praise well.

As a young boy, when I became old enough to understand that I did not live with my mother, but was being raised by my grandmother, I was deeply affected. I loved and appreciated my grandmother for loving me and taking care of me. But I knew a tiny bit about life and one thing I knew was that something was not quite right about a child not being raised by his mother when his mother was able to do so. Our family never discussed why I was being raised by my grandmother and not my mother. If they ever talked about it, it was out of my hearing and they surely never talked to me about it. I was a happy child who was well taken care of, but my six and seven-year-old brain could not make sense of it all. In the way that only a child could reason, I deduced that it would not take much to remove me from the familiar environment and the people I loved. I had convinced myself that if I wasn't a good child or if I made any trouble at all for my grandmother, I actually might end up being raised by someone else. The fact that many of the children with which I went to school were indeed not being raised by their parents or were in foster homes only bolstered that anxiety. Just like they had never explained why my mother was not currently raising me, I just assumed that there would be no explanation as to why someone else would suddenly become my guardian.

In my little mind, I just assumed that I must have been burdensome as a baby – too much crying or drinking too much milk or needing to be changed too often – that caused my mother to choose to have my grandmother raise me. Unsure of exactly how that scenario might actually again play itself out, I took every possible precaution not to stir up trouble or cause any inconvenience. I always did what I was told. I excelled in school. I rarely asked for things. I learned to make do with what was easily available. For some warped reason, I concluded that being praised or celebrated or talked about too much could also trigger "the unknown thing" that would place me in the care and keeping of another person. I did not want that to happen.

I wish that our family had talked to each other more and especially to me. It is not true that I was an introverted child – I was anything but. It is true that I turned inside more often than was healthy or appropriate. I was always reluctant to ask for help when I needed it. I think I felt guilty at having been a sickly child and I was completely aware of all that my grandmother had to do to take care of me. The sacrifices she had to make were great in the context that we lived. In my mind, the only possible thing that I could do to recompense her for her sacrifices for me was to make sure I didn't cause her any pain or frustration or unnecessary time or expense. It was almost as if I kept a ledger recording every act of kindness that the world offered me and the only credit I could post to the account was finding a way of not being a burden to the world.

So as a child, my Christmas list was always very short. I practiced acting as if I never really wanted anything. This deception, I thought, would not put my grandmother at the disadvantage of having to get whatever my secret desire was. I spent most of my play time to myself often believing that getting the adults to play with me would be some grand imposition on them. I know that I was loved as a child. I had a wonderfully caring guardian in my grandmother who always made sure I had the essentials of life. But we were not the kind of people who showed very much emotion toward each other nor did we express our feelings of love well. However, children need that kind of affirming affection and expressed love. While I regret that I did not get that as a child, I have been very intentional about being expressive in my love for others as an adult. My own childhood taught me that.

I had begun to grow out of that when I reached my teens. The ultimate "me celebrating" thing to do was to ask my grandmother if I could have a cookout for my sixteenth birthday. I had never had a birthday party before as I could remember. There may well have been small commemorations of my birthday: a cake baked or a toy bought or a call from a relative who lived far away. But I had never had a "real" party. The only reason I knew that such a thing even existed was that I occasionally was invited to one being held for one of my friends. Asking for a birthday party was such a strange request coming from me that my grandmother set no limits. She went all out. She was determined to make my birthday almost as big as my "trial" sermon had been a year earlier. She had a new basketball goal installed in the yard so my friends could play. Such an important day required the purchase of a new grill. The old picnic table was re-painted and spruced up by a neighbor for the event. I was told to invite whomever I wanted and, after weeks of adding to and crossing off names from a guest list, eighteen other teenagers had been invited to my party.

It was a picture perfect April day for an outdoor birthday party. The grass had been cut and the yard had been appropriately manicured for my big day. The food was beautiful in presentation and plenteous in quantity. A portable turntable had been borrowed from somebody and the perfectly selected 45s had been neatly piled by the music machine on a corner of the concrete front porch. I did not sleep a wink the night before. It was a picture perfect day and I could not wait for my invited guests to arrive. The hour for the party to begin came and went as did many others, but no one came.

Quietly and without a word of consolation or explanation, my grandmother came out of the house as the sun was beginning to set. She busied herself with wrapping up uneaten food and gathering up the stacks of records that had gone un-played that afternoon. I watched it all from a position seated at my basketball goal, my back to the pole that had been erected in the rich soil of our Virginia home, and the brand new basketball in my lap. When she was done, she called out to me from the back door and said "Happy Birthday." The exclamation point to her birthday wish was the empty sound of the screen door being released and slamming shut.

I did not cry, but I was overwhelmed with the sadness I felt at having caused so much trouble, time and expense to my grandmother. I did not process the fact that transportation had always been a problem in our small, rural county. Many of my invited guests simply had no way to travel the miles to our house. As teenagers, most of my friends had a job of some kind. If it was not a "public" job (that is, a job working for a store or a company), many had jobs working on the family farm. In most instances, a whole day to have a party was much too frivolous a waste of valuable time that could be spent on farm chores. Had I thought of any of these things, I would have planned an event much better suited to the particulars of the time, place and circumstance of my life, my friends and our world. I thought only of what I wanted and I sincerely believed that I had caused great injury to the one person in the world who loved me most.

Again, if only our family had been able to talk to each other, but we all lacked the skills and tools so to do. It was clear that we loved each other, but it was rarely said. We enjoyed each other's affection, but it was rarely shown. We were content to try to figure out how the others felt, what they thought and how they might react. We preferred guessing what another would like or dislike. Talking about it was not our preferred method. It never occurred to us that simply talking about things and talking to each other would have solved a multitude of problems. I did not know how to talk about how I felt about that April day that began so sunny and warm, but descended into darkness and despair. I internalized it all and said nothing. The only way I could process what the appropriate penance would be was to resolve to never again celebrate me.

Out of the twenty-four years that I was a pastor, I only celebrated the annual pastor's anniversary four times. There were three such events over my seventeen years at Shady Grove and one event in my seven years at Temple Memorial. After that "sweet sixteen" birthday party, I would not have another party until I was 42. It actually turned out to be more of a celebration for other people I loved and respected. I rented limousines, made reservations for a dinner at an exclusive restaurant, had prime seats at a theatre to see a play and rented an entire restaurant after closing hours to have dessert after the play. It was a splendid and expensive affair that I paid for myself. The invitations noted "gifts are not required and will not be accepted."

I went eight months following my call to my pastorate in High Point before I would submit to having an installation service. Part of the reason was I was so unsure of whether I would succeed at this church; part of the reason was I would have to endure an entire day about me. When I came to my current position of denominational executive, it was marked by no commemorative event: no banquet, no worship service, no installation program, no engraved announcements sent to friends and supporters, no press releases in the newspapers. Nothing. It was likely an oversight in light of the chaos that surrounded my ascension to that office. I did not complain at all. Coming in without fanfare was perfectly fine with me. I was actually relieved.

I have never been one to too quickly embrace the idea that negative events in our lives are authored by God. I recognize that this might sometimes be the case, but I tend to conclude that "time and chance happeneth" to all. Rarely have I seen the signature of God on the dark parts of my journey in ministry. Yet I have been unmovable in my belief that the hand of God can be present in those dark places as God uses the negative things in life to shape us for His service. It may be that God looks for the dark places in our living and lights a candle there. While He is not responsible for the darkness, He is the one Who has the candle and match.

My discomfort with being praised and celebrated is something that is deeply rooted in my psyche and self-image. I likely would have benefited from professional counseling somewhere on my journey. The events I described previously have left me scarred. Notice that I said "scarred." I did not say "wounded." There is a wide span between the two. A wound hurts. A wound requires constant attention. A wound is the gateway through which infections enter that can destroy the whole body. However, a scar is a wound that has been healed. A scar hurts no more. A scar requires no attention. The scab on a scar is a vault door that keeps the bad things out.

I am sure that there is some reason in medicine as to why some wounds leave scars and others do not. On a spiritual plane, I have come to understand why some of our hurts in life leave scars and others do not. I believe that any scar that life leaves on the spirit of a Christian is left there as a reminder and a testimony. It is a reminder to the Christian of some lesson, some purpose, some meaning that God has for your life; to others who are wounded, and a scar is the testimony that God does heal.

The hardest thing for a Christian to do, in my opinion, is to embrace and live out the meaning of Luke 9:23: *"And he said to them all, If any man will come after me, let him deny himself, and take up his cross daily, and follow me."* The hard part is not the coming after Jesus, the taking up of the cross, nor the following. The hard part is what must precede these things: denying self.

Selfishness, I have come to believe, is the rich soil out of which sin takes root and grows. Selfishness feeds and nurtures sin until sin, like the uncontrollable kudzu, takes over. Choose whatever malady you believe to negatively affect the heart of humanity and you will discover some inflated sense of self therein that diminishes the love for others. Perhaps this is why Jesus calls on us to love others as we love ourselves. He knows how strong the love of self can be. I am not suggesting that a person should not have self-love nor am I suggesting that a Christian empty themselves of any of the instincts to take care of and protect one's self. The first is unhealthy and the second impossible. What I am suggesting is that the call to follow Christ and be true to one's calling will inevitably and unavoidably demand sacrifice – a denying of what I may want for what Christ wants of me. The ability to live a self-denying life is critically important to finding progress on the path of the never ending transformation that makes us Christian. Before a person can truly come after Christ, the person must be willing to place their wants on the shelf lower than the shelf of what Christ wants from us. Before a person can truly daily take up a cross of service and ministry, the person must know how to deny one's self. Before a person can become a follower of Christ, the person must practice self-denial.

I refuse to believe that my humiliation in Mrs. Pope's fifth grade class nor my painful sixteenth birthday party were part and parcel of God's plan for my life. They both seem out of character to me considering what I know and love about God. I do know that the best intentions, for whatever reasons, sometime bring disastrous results. As well, the plans of people and rodents can easily go wrong. But I do believe that the scarring that resulted from both of these events have been my motivation (and my reminder) to live a life accustomed to self-denial. The praise that I do not wish for myself I have learned to heap on others. The attention that I would not prefer for myself is exactly what I like to bring to others. My sense of not wanting to be a burden to other people makes me not complain when others bring their burdens to me.

Self-denial, however, is not a state that one reaches. It is a constant pursuit. Every day, I am confronted with the choice of serving God and others or fulfilling my own selfish desires. I grant that the grace of self-denial is all the harder when I am overworked, overburdened and overtaxed in so many other ways. It is easy to say "to hell with everybody else. It is all about me!" Admittedly, there are times when that is what I say, how I feel and how I act. It is then that I need desperately to remember my scar.

Self-denial comes easier when it is practiced alongside humility. To me, humility is not a wilted flower nor does it make for a person who is easily manipulated or walked upon. It is closely akin to what Paul had on his mind when he advised that a person should *"not to think of himself more highly than he ought to think."* Humility has a lot to do with the concept that it is not all about me.

I have a very large personality and that comes coupled with a strong sense of confidence. I know my presence in a room can be overpowering if I choose so to be. I have not been a stranger to being cocky. For me, the practice of humility is acutely important. Just as the athlete has to endure hard training and practice before the big game, I too have to practice the grace of being humble before the big game of ministry. Over the years, this grace has become more and more comfortable to me. For that, I am grateful indeed.

I am alarmed, however, at the swelling tides of arrogance, self-importance and self-absorption so apparent in modern ministry today. The age of the celebrity preacher is unquestionably upon us. Fewer and fewer popular preachers see themselves and their Christian work as an extension of the ministry of the Church but rather as CEOs of their own ministry enterprises. In some instances, the church appears only to be an additional marketing tool for books, recordings and webpages that seem to bring less to the glory of God and more to the vanity of a preacher. Excellence in ministry will naturally bring attention and perhaps even adoration from the people who find help and hope in one's ministry. But just because the people bring it, it does not mean that you have to accept it or encourage it.

Arrogance has become so widely acceptable that fellowship among preachers and cooperation among churches is becoming rarer. I might be able to understand arrogance from a minister who has had a long career peppered with various successes and notable accomplishments. While I don't agree with that, at least I can understand that. However, I am seeing more preachers in the first years of their ministry – without a singular accomplishment to which they can point – showing arrogance and pride. How unfortunate that is indeed! I live and work in Raleigh, the capital city of North Carolina. It is not uncommon for pastors in other metropolitan areas of the state to call me to find out what is going on in churches in the city where they serve and reside. They are too arrogant to admit that they are interested in their sisters' and brothers' work by talking directly to their colleagues. They prefer to have me interpose on their behalf.

There are pastors who do rule their churches out of fear and intimidation. They routinely humiliate the members to keep them in line and on the expected pathway. It is not uncommon for them to chastise their adversaries publicly. They play a dangerous game of choosing favorites among equals and then they hold the prized favored status over their heads threatening to take it away on a whim. As easily and quickly as the favored ones achieved that lofty status, they can as easily and quickly lose that status and be relegated to a place far from favor and influence. I call this a game because it is rigged to ensure that the only winner is that pastor who rakes in the Monopoly money of power and control. In the process, hearts are broken and confidence in ministry collapses. The days of earning influence and authority in the church by virtue of hard work, committed labor, and faithful service are long and sadly gone. Now ministers expect to enter their ministry on the first day with the same authority as their colleagues have who have been "on the battlefield" for decades. When conflict inevitably arise, these preaching rookies automatically assume that the problem is the people. They never consider the possibility that their approach to ministry and service has been entirely wrong.

I wish Christian leaders would be honest about this one thing: not every idea for ministry is a vision straight from the heart of God. God uses our intellect, experience and judgment in determining the courses of our ministries. Of course, He does speak, but the decision to change the color of the church's trash cans from black to green does not rise to the level of Divine annunciation. God can trust you on that one. Yet there are ministers who try to convince those that they serve that their personal preference is the sure and certain and unchangeable plan of God to be neither questioned nor challenged. However, these ministers forget that spiritual people have a spiritual sense about the things of God as well. My ministry has been advanced over the years simply because I had a good idea. That idea may have resulted from something I read, something I heard, something I witnessed or something that I simply figured out for myself. I would have done a disservice to God to declare it to have been some great and glorious "move of God" when it was just the use of commonsense. Thanks be to God that He gives us commonsense as well. Manipulation of people who love you and who respect your ministry is a sin that grows straight from the soil of an inflated sense of self. It should be quickly cut down. Save the pronouncements about having heard the voice of God specifically for those instances where God has pressed Himself so firmly upon your spirit. Framing routine decision in as regal a garment as the certain will of God will lead the spiritual people in your midst to accuse you of too often "crying wolf" when no such thing is present or imminent.

Perhaps these ministers – the arrogant, the self-centered, and the power hungry – have wounds from their own lives that never became scars. Perhaps they lost their way in the maze that is ministry. Perhaps they were not fortunate to have the kind of role models to shape their ministry while it was still pliable and without final form. Perhaps it is a quirk in their personality. Perhaps it is something more deeply personal, painful and perhaps even more malevolent than I am willing to consider. I really don't know.

To ensure that I would not lean too heavily in that direction, I have tried to practice humility throughout the course of my ministry. I have tried to set these small reminders in my day-to-day world to keep me focused more on what is really important and less on me, myself, and I. That trio can push the best intentioned minister off the path of service onto an expressway that leads to sure destruction. In my parish ministry, I refused to allow my name to go in any of the normal places: not on the outdoor signage, not on the church letterhead, not on the church vans. I did finally agree to add my name to the message board in the vestibule of my first church, but only after insisting that the phrase "Jesus Christ, Head of the Church" be positioned above "Haywood T. Gray, Pastor." Some members thought I was embarrassed to be affiliated with the church, but that was not at all the case. I was simply sending signals to myself that it is more about Christ, about Christ's church, and about Christ's people than it was about me.

When invited to other churches to preach, I never sit at the host pastor's desk – even if offered. When entering the sanctuary of a church where I have been invited, I like to follow the host pastor into the pulpit instead of walking out first. I wait to be invited to sit in the center seat even though I know in my heart that is the proper place for the guest speaker. I detest long introductions and when asked what I would like said of me, I usually respond that my preference would be to introduce me by giving my name and my job title. That's enough. I sometimes arrive for services that I am not on the program late so as not to have to sit up front or in the pulpit. I try to be comfortable wherever I am. All these little inducements tend to keep me focused and humble.

I wish I could say that I am a master at self-denial and humility. I certainly am not. I remember naming myself "Senior Pastor" in my first Church. I did not ask the church to do so, I just placed it on the front of the bulletin and had a new name plate designed for my office door. The funny thing about it was that I didn't have to name myself "senior" pastor or any other kind of pastor. I was the ONLY pastor. My entire staff consisted of me, a part-time secretary and an even more part-time custodian. Not another minister, pastor or preacher was to be found for miles around. Still I took on the title "Senior Pastor." While that title fed my ego, it did not enhance the ministry of Jesus Christ in any way whatsoever. Fortunately, the kind people of that parish were aware that I was young and dumb and they did not chastise me for that error.

Even now I do enjoy the perks that come with my job as a leader of our denomination in North Carolina. I admit that there are times that I like seeing my name in a favorable newspaper article. I have been known to enjoy having a position of influence where I could make an event or an organization change course and direction simply because of my input. I have been known to be totally bewildered why subordinates could not understand why my idea or suggestion was not the best idea since the invention of red Kool-Aid. I confess that I am far from being a perfect man or a perfect Christian. But it is true that I work really hard on being less arrogant, on not being so self-absorbed and on putting the needs of others before my frivolous wants and desires. The older I get, the more likely I am to find little ways to remind myself of these kinds of things that begin as minor bumps in the road but, unchecked, can devolve into major potholes.

If Mrs. Pope was the reason for one of the greatest humiliations in my young life, she was also the bringer of the best hope I had had for success. Six years after her fifth grade classroom, she would be the one who brought me to the lifeline in ministry that I so desperately needed. And that lifeline was J. W. Brown.

Lessons for Ministry

1. Be very careful of your health during your ministry. Attend to both your physical health and your mental health. I regret that I did very little of either. The stresses and demands of ministry in the modern context takes a toll on the body as well as the mind. Diet, exercise, and rest are very important parts to the

mix that makes a minister whole. Do not neglect your mental health. Getting away, hobbies, entertainment and friends are all necessary ingredients for good mental health. When ministry and life become weighty, consider getting help from mental health professionals. To do so is no admission of failure or inadequacy. It is the wise action of a person who wants to offer God their best selves for God's work and witness.

2. Practice humility. There will always be more people cheering for you in ministry than there will be people coaching you in ministry. If you choose to only hear the cheers, you may fall victim to arrogance, excessive pride and envy. Find little things that will remind you of the grace of humility. Strategically place those little things in the corners of your life so that you will be reminded and encouraged.

3. Never underestimate how the pain in your life can become a part of your passion in ministry. Pray for healing for your hurts, but also pray that God will somehow use your injuries to make a difference in the lives of others.

CHAPTER 8

"LORD, SHOW ME THE WAY"

S IX YEARS AFTER leaving Mrs. Pope's fifth grade reading class, she re-entered my world. By this time, the "Junior Pastor" position at Bryant's was turning into more of a burden than a joy. My relationship with the pastor who signed my license to preach was quickly deteriorating. I am not exactly sure why we weren't getting along. We grew more and more distant and he gave me fewer and fewer learning assignments. I always felt that one contributing factor to the growing crevice in our father-in-ministry/son-in-ministry relationship was my growing popularity. A teenage preacher was an oddity and people wanted to see the curiosity. I knew that I was not growing in ministry and there was so much that I did not know nor very much that I understood. In addition to all of this, my grandmother had been diagnosed with cancer and the treatments designed to cure her often made her feel worse. This was the beginning of multiple hospitalizations and long recovery periods for her. At this time, it was only the two of us at home and I had to take on more and more of the responsibilities to keep the household going. With these additional responsibility, there was no time left for learning about ministry. About all I could do was keep up with my school work and get the housework done.

I do not remember exactly how I came to ride with Mrs. Pope to her church. I don't remember if I asked her, if she asked my grandmother's permission or if it was all happenstance. Mrs. Pope was a member of Shiloh Baptist Church in Boykins, Virginia. Shiloh was the church of great renown in our county. Anybody who was somebody was likely a member of Shiloh. It was larger than most other churches in the county and it was literally filled to the rafters on Sundays. The ground floor and balcony were packed far beyond capacity on most Sundays. Their music ministry was distinctive in many ways. While most churches had only an upright piano (rarely tuned or in "playing shape"), Shiloh had both a piano and an organ. I think I had never heard an organ play in a church before Shiloh. I could not believe that such music was of an earthly origin. It seemed as if there was always something going on at Shiloh. While my home church had worship twice a month, Sunday school every Sunday, quarterly church conference and Revival once a year, Shiloh had its doors open every Sunday and at least three or four days a week. For our community, you could not do better than Shiloh.

Reverend J. W. Brown was Shiloh's pastor. He was fair complexioned like me, but that's where the comparison ended. Tall and an elegant presence in the pulpit, Rev. Brown was always immaculately dressed. His crisp, white shirts never seemed to wrinkle. Dust was afraid to stick to his shoes that were always polished to a high gloss. He chose the perfect jewelry and accessories to whatever suit he was wearing. His ties added a splash of color and an affirmation of his keen sense of style. He was never flashy, but he was definitely a head turner. The women swooned over him and the men wanted to be like him.

At seventeen, I did not know very much at all about the inner workings of a church, but it was quite apparent that Rev. Brown had created a well-oiled machine at Shiloh. While worship service at Bryant's began whenever enough people showed up, the Call to Worship at Shiloh was always given at exactly 11:00 a.m. While the choirs at Mars Hill generally sang whatever had been last rehearsed during choir practice, the music at Shiloh was carefully chosen to compliment the sermon or the theme for the day. The ushers at churches in the area behaved as if they were independent contractors – everyone doing their own thing. However, the Shiloh ushers worked as one organism with neat uniforms, flawless precision and perfect collaboration. Shiloh had it going on!

Rev. Brown had quite a reputation as a preacher. Whenever I heard him preach, I was inspired and motivated. He was the kind of preacher that I wanted to be. In my seventeen-year-old mind, I never thought that I could become the pastor of a great church like Shiloh. After hearing Reverend Brown, my resolve was to learn to preach as if I had a great church like Shiloh. His preaching style was certain, but never quite predictable. If you followed the text that he was preaching, you could assume what direction he might take, but he was known to bring a surprise or two. It became almost fun to try to figure out what he might say before he said it. I mostly lost that game, however. He was one of a handful of preachers that I knew at the time who took care to explain the text that he was preaching. He told his listeners about the context of the Scripture that he was preaching. He always found a way to make what he was preaching relevant. He was a great storyteller and his words splashed on the empty canvas that was my mind as if Michelangelo was present with color palate and brushes. He did it all. He taught some; he made us think some; he challenged us some; he preached us into a frenzy some.

Mrs. Pope started picking me up for church more and more often and Reverend Brown took a liking to me. While Sunday school was going on (Mrs. Pope was one of Shiloh's Sunday school teachers), Reverend Brown would keep me cloistered in his study conducting a kind of school for me. He taught me how to use a Bible concordance. He showed me the value of the footnotes, maps and margin notes of the Scofield Reference Bible that had been presented to me when I was licensed. I discovered, in great amazement, that there were more versions of the Bible than the one that King James had commissioned. I had come to think that either by the Gospel itself or at least by federal law, God just had to speak using "thee's" and "thine's" before Reverend Brown taught me otherwise.

It wasn't very long after I started showing up at Shiloh that Rev. Brown invited me to preach. However, preaching there was no simple endeavor. It was a three-week ordeal. The first week, I would have to bring my sermon manuscript on Sunday and, while Sunday school was going on, he would critique it and offer suggestions on it. The following Sunday, I would have to present my revisions and he would make sure I had included the changes he'd told me about. Often he would lend books to me out of his personal library to take home to read about the text I was planning to preach. If I did not get something correct, he would declare that I had not done my reading. Most of the time, he was right. On the third Sunday after receiving the preaching assignment, I would stand in the Shiloh pulpit to preach.

I was simply amazed at the transformation. Previously, I had sensed that people were only watching me preach. With Rev. Brown's tutelage, I felt that people were actually listening to me preach. More than that, they seemed genuinely interested in what I had to say. (Rev. Brown had convinced me to semi-retire the red cape. I never wore it at Shiloh, but I did don it for afternoon services at other churches.)

When I wasn't preparing for a sermon with Rev. Brown's help, we would spend our Sunday school time together talking about preaching. These interchanges were so helpful. There was never an agenda. He would just tell me something he'd learned about preaching and I would pepper him with questions. He would talk and I would make mental notes. Preaching, to Rev. Brown, was sacred and serious so he helped rid me of all the showmanship that had become my trademark. He broke the habit of leaving the pulpit and heading for the back door while preaching. He convinced me that people could be moved to shout when the preacher stood flat-footed behind the pulpit. (At first, I did not actually believe that until I saw him do it.) He explained that the power of a good sermon was in the fact that it was a good sermon.

I never knew very much about Rev. Brown's personal life. As the county's leading preacher, there were the unavoidable rumors whispered about him. I never really got to know his family well nor did I ever set foot in his home. We never discussed the other dimensions of being a pastor and church administration never crossed his lips. With him and me, it was all about preaching. In a way of saying thank you to him, I did as much as I could to imitate him and follow his instructions. For the first time in my young ministry did I feel hopeful that I might actually make something of being a minister. I was grateful that I crossed paths with J. W. Brown and he taught me some very valuable lessons that would bolster my own preaching ministry across the years. Without his instruction, I would have floundered as a preacher. If J. W. Brown taught me to value preaching, Arthur R. White taught me how to value doing ministry and to love the work of the church.

Averett College (now University) was the place where I would go through the rite of passage from youth to adulthood. I was not that much anxious about living away from home for the first time. My large concern was not having the safe harbor of a church in my life. I am not exactly sure how the information came to me, but I was convinced that I would find a church home at Loyal Baptist Church in Danville, Virginia, I never made the requisite student visit to campus so I had no clue as to what college life at Averett would be nor what kind of adventures the city of Danville had in store for me. I was taking it all in faith. I figured that so long as my soul would have a resting place in a church home, I was not that concerned about where my body would dwell for the next few years.

I arrived on the crowded and chaotic freshman weekend. After becoming vaguely familiar with the college campus, I set out to find Loyal. The Loyal Church was just over a mile from my college campus on the famed Holbrook Street. Holbrook Street had once been the African-American business and social hub of the city. In its day, Holbrook Street would be where the principals, funeral homes, doctors, lawyers and churches were located. By the time I arrived in 1978, much of the former glory had begun to fade, but one could easily tell how this hallowed street had once been a place of the privileged and the powerful.

I did not have a car and knew nothing of the concept of public transportation so I set out on foot in the hot August sun to find the location of Loyal. I wanted to know exactly where it was and to time my walk there so I would not risk being late the first Sunday I would show up for worship. I was also hopeful that I might meet the minister so I could make myself known to him. That first walk to Loyal was one of the most interesting trips of my young life. I passed Sacred Heart Catholic Church. I knew of no such people in our rural Southampton County. In the next block was a Lutheran congregation. Not long after I came across Mount Vernon United Methodist Church. I was beginning to wonder if Baptists were in exile like John on Patmos. The route I took passed Danville Memorial Hospital (where I would later work as a medical social worker) and the Last Capital of the Confederacy. This Museum to the last place where President Jefferson Davis presided over the confederate states was strangely positioned at the intersection of Main Street and Holbrook Street. I thought it odd (and actually quite funny) that a memorial to the slave holding confederates would stand as the gateway to the city's most prominent and prized black neighborhoods. I would later take great delight in that irony.

When I arrived at Loyal, I was awestruck. It was mammoth in size and had the most beautiful stained glass windows I had ever seen. Even the fabled Shiloh Baptist Church of Boykins paled in comparison to this place. Unfortunately, neither the minister nor a custodian was there so I could not see the inside. I was so excited about getting the opportunity to worship there. In my mind, I was already imagining preaching in such an impressive building. Danville, I thought, was going to be all right.

On my first Sunday in Danville, I rose early, had breakfast in the college cafeteria and dressed in my best (and only) suit and set off to begin life as a member of Loyal Baptist Church. However, the hot August sun is one thing when wearing shorts, tee shirt and running shoes. It is quite another thing in suit and jacket, shirt and tie and Church shoes that always look much better than they feel on the feet. What had been a nice stroll a few days earlier was turning into an Olympic-like track and field event in the hot summer sun with full Sunday preaching uniform on. By the time I reached Holbrook Street, I was tired and thirsty. I had started to contemplate if my first Danville worship experience should have been in a Catholic Church seeing that they were a mere two blocks from the campus. I had not noticed Calvary Baptist Church on my previous scouting trip to find Loyal, but there she stood – like an oasis in the desert. The sign said "Baptist" and I could hear the glorious and inviting whine of the air conditioning units churning in battle with the August heat. I could get to Loyal on another Sunday. This place would do for today.

I entered the lower level which led to a fellowship hall and various classrooms. I asked someone for the location of the men's room and then asked someone where I might find the pastor. I was directed to a staircase at the back of the lower level and moved in that direction. Before ascending the stairwell, I noticed a man standing at the top of the stairs. He was striking in his appearance. He was tall, fit, very well groomed with a modern dark suit and crisp white shirt. Like me, he had a neatly trimmed afro that I assumed he sported all of the time. On the contrary, my afro could be classified as neat only because I'd gotten a haircut before leaving home to begin my adventure in college. I didn't have a clue who he was, but if chic and cool people like him were members of this Church, I could see myself abandoning Loyal for Calvary.

Wanting to be sure that I was headed in the right direction, I asked him where I might find the pastor. His response was simple and shocking, "I am the pastor," It took me a while to fully comprehend the possibility of a cool dude like this – only ten or so years my senior – could be the pastor of a "real" church like Calvary, I bounded up the steps to introduce myself and he extended a hand to me. I condensed my short life into a thirty second commercial. When he found out that I was a freshman student and a minister, he smiled broadly and invited me into his office. That would be the first of so many days spent under his tutelage and in his office.

The really shocking thing about walking into Rev. White's study was that it was an actual study. There were books everywhere. It was clear that he spent time there and clear that his time spent there was consumed with reading and writing. The good pastor apparently loved both. The conversation was meaningful as he was very interested in knowing about me. He did not converse with me as his inferior (as so many older ministers had done with me over the years), he spoke with me as colleague choosing to address me as Reverend and not by my first name.

I could not get over how much confidence he exuded. It was as if he were born for this day and every other day that came. In a sense, I was feeling a bit intimidated by my brand new world. I was excited about being in college and excited about becoming a city dweller. My excitement was tempered by the sheer audacity of how much my life was about to change. I think I needed a boost of confidence and The Reverend White would certainly provide that. When you are unsure of yourself, being around people who are self-confident helps to build your confidence. Within thirty minutes of having met Rev. White, I was on my way toward believing that I would soon have the world swinging on a chain.

Calvary was unlike any other church in which I had worshipped. Its worship would be considered "high church" compared to the country chapels in which I had spent my youth. Worship was quieter than I was used to and the music was dominated by hymns and anthems. I had been partially introduced to that kind of music at Shiloh, but it was nothing as majestic as it was at Calvary. It was here that I learned to love the hymns and anthems. I took to the hymnal with a vengeance and was determined to learn the lyrics to as many as I possibly could. There were a good number of professional people in Calvary just as there had been in Shiloh, but the Calvary people impressed me with their dignity and gravitas. I would later learn that many people in the community thought Calvary to be a "stuck up" church, but I never thought that. They were my new family and, while entirely different from the family I was born into, they accepted me with open arms.

My skills as a preacher grew considerably under Rev. White's instruction and interest in me, but he impacted my ministry greatest by exposing me to the work of the church and the concept of ministry. Prior to my time in Danville, I had only considered ministry be the sermon on Sunday morning. I had not seen the holistic ministry of the church. Rev. White helped me to see ministry as a way of life and as an acceptable answer to the call of God. While I had only been involved in Christian education ministries back home, a whole new world was opening to me at Calvary. Missions, evangelism, and outreach were among the new words I was learning and living. I was given an assignment on the prison ministry team and I would periodically head a small worship team that would lead worship in the local city detention center. I honed my preaching skills at these Sunday afternoon events. More than being their visiting preacher, I was learning what counseling was about as Rev.

White encouraged me to visit the inmates and share my testimony as they shared theirs. It was a powerful exercise in developing a thirst to do ministry in a relevant context.

The Calvary Church had a reputation of being a difficult church to lead. Rev. White rarely shared with me the struggles of the pastorate. He would occasionally discuss some conflict in the church, but never just for the sake of venting his frustration, but he always had an eye toward walking me through the process of resolving conflicts, understanding their root and origin and never being defeated by ministry's difficulties. He and Mrs. White would have me over to their house for dinner and, after the meal, he and I would have these broad and deep discussions about theology, about the church, and about life. A product of Virginia Union University's School of Theology, Rev. White was a deep thinker. He challenged me to think deeply as well. Rarely did I gain the upper hand in our discussions and debates, but the object was never to win – the objective was to have thought deeply about something. Learning to think deeply, he believed, would make for deep thought in preaching. Not only did Rev. White's tutelage lead me to think deeply about preaching, but it made me think deeply about life. I became much more methodical in my decision-making processes. While I tend not to hesitate when it comes to making a decision, I often have played out scenarios of what I might do in a variety of situations. When something similar occurs, I have already weighed my options. Some of that comes from years of playing alone as a youth and some of it was perfected under Rev. White's ministry to me. One very helpful thing that he would have me do was this: if we attended any kind of event together, he would ask me when it was over what I may have said or done had I been on the program. I began a habit of both listening and thinking while others were presenting: listening to what they had to say while, at the same time, thinking about what I might say were I in their shoes. Over the years, one files away countless scenarios and situations and, with a fairly good memory, one can bring up appropriate remarks on a moment's notice.

Thinking through things has served me well in ministry. I spend a lot of time thinking – perhaps more than I should. I do not play chess, but I have heard that the successful chess master must think through a myriad of possible moves before making a move. Ministry is fairly akin to something on that wise. I learned a lot from the good Reverend White and I owe him more than I will ever be able to repay. If Rev. J W. Brown taught me to love preaching and if Reverend Arthur R. White taught me to love the church and its work, then The Reverend Dr. Eugene Burns Turner would teach me almost everything else I know.

Almost two years after assuming my first pastorate in North Carolina, I attended the first Baptist state convention that I had ever attended. I had been introduced to the concept of state conventions when I was a member of Calvary Church in Danville. They were members of the famed Baptist General Convention of Virginia and Calvary was one of their prized congregations. However, I never felt any particular passion for denominational work although Rev. White was careful to keep me abreast of the Convention's work.

Queen Esther Blackwell was a member of my first church and she was downright worrisome about my getting involved in the work of the denomination on the state level. I was active in our local Association, but the state convention did not necessarily interest me at this point in my ministry. Just as you do things that you don't necessarily want to do for the folk in your family that you love, so do you do for the folk in your church who love you. I agreed to attend the 1982 Annual Session of the General Baptist State Convention of North Carolina, Inc. convening at the famed White Rock Baptist Church in Durham, North Carolina. It was a presidential election year for the convention, but I barely had any interest in that. I just wanted to be in a grand church like White Rock.

The White Rock Baptist Church is a monumental stone building standing guard over Fayetteville Street in Durham. It is a short distance from North Carolina Central University. Fayetteville Street's famed history is similar to what had been the case in Danville on Holbrook Street. The legendary Miles Mark Fisher – educator, professor, pastor, and theologian – had been the pastor of White Rock and the late Dr. Fisher had achieved near sainthood among most North Carolina Baptist preachers of prominence at that time. To be in the building was a special treat for me. I had figured that I could endure the pain of a state convention meeting (in which I had very little interest) so long as the meeting was being held at a place like White Rock.

Neither I nor the church I served had money for things like a hotel room or a meal allowance. The church did muster up enough for registration and for gas. Since Durham was only an hour's drive, I commuted each day. I tried to arrive early – before registration opened. Before the daily call to order, I would do what all young preachers in the dawn of their ministries would do. I would wander the halls of White Rock's grand building and pretend that I was the pastor making the morning rounds. I poked my head in vacant rooms and spoke to non-existent staff persons whom I imagined were taking their orders for the day from me. I spent a good portion of my first day at the Convention trying to figure out some way to weasel myself into the pastor's office of the Reverend Dr. Lorenzo D. Lynch, the church's current pastor. I did meet Dr. Lynch and had the chance to speak very briefly with him. I never did muster up the courage to ask if I could see his office and sit at his desk. The thought did keep coming back to my mind though. The grandeur of White Rock and the sheer delight at being at my first Convention was almost too much for a twenty-two-year-old pastor still very much wet behind the ears. I saw the program filled with the names of prominent ministers that I had met or heard about, but none of whom I considered colleagues or associates. I fear that when I returned to my own parish,

I likely dropped too many names and left too many inferences that I was "tight" with some people who only shook my hand while passing through a crowd.

Wednesday was the big, election day. I returned early to the site, but found that I was by no means the only early arriver. Busses, vans, and cars of all types have claimed every possible piece of land that was White Rock's property. I was forced to find a seat in the balcony. Although I was mesmerized by the crowd and by the noticeable tension in the atmosphere, I was not very interested in what was going on. Dr. J. R. Manley (who was the outgoing president) did a tremendous job in delivering his final address/sermon. I was impressed, but as soon as the lunch break was announced, I was off to my preferred preoccupation: wandering the halls of the church seeing what goes on in a place like White Rock.

The two main contenders for the Presidency that year were The Reverend Dr. J. B. Humphrey of the First Baptist Church-West in Charlotte, NC and The Reverend E. Burns Turner of First Baptist Church of Lumberton, NC. I knew nothing of convention politics and could not have cared less. However, our local Association had endorsed Dr. Humphrey so I was content to cast my vote for him and find a nearby McDonald's where a poor Baptist preacher could eat and have something left over for the gasoline needed for the return trip home. When I returned to the White Rock campus, I decided to ditch the afternoon session and return to my now habit-forming practice of wandering the halls.

The Reverend Dr. E. L. Kirby was Moderator of my local Association and I came upon him unexpectedly in the hallway. I quickly pretended to be headed somewhere as I saw him first. I did not want my Baptist leader to know that I had pretty much become a goof-off. When Dr. Kirby saw me, he came to me in an almost frenzied way that I was not accustomed to coming from him. He told me that something had gone amiss with a person who was to have served as a teller for Dr. Humphrey and he needed me to fill-in and be a teller for Dr. Humphrey. Before I could ask a single question, I was ushered into a room in the bowels of the Church into a scenario about which I had no clue what was going on.

I had gained special access to the counting room. Here all the ballots were brought to be counted by hand. (This was pre-voting machine days.) This room was as close to a smoke-filled back room of a mobster's hideout as I could imagine – sans the smoke and the mobsters. I later found out that my presence was needed to ensure that no shenanigans took place (not that I knew what shenanigans I should look for) and to periodically exit the count room to report to Dr. Kirby how the vote was going. Being greener than an unripe banana, I always reported to Dr. Kirby that everything was going well and we were ahead. I really didn't have a clue whether either was the case. Seeing that I was a "boy" pastor with no experience or reputation, I was pretty much regarded like I was a plastic plant in the corner of the room. Thanks be to God that Dr. Humphrey had other tellers in the room. It wasn't too long before I picked up on agreeing with whatever the other Humphrey tellers objected to. I wasn't smart enough to spot out any shenanigans on my own, but I was willing to agree with any shenanigans spotted by others in the room.

E. B. Turner won the election in an after-midnight runoff. I was tired and just ready to get home. I did not have a hotel room so I would have to drive a little over an hour to find rest in my own bed. Basically, I was done with conventioneering and decided that I would not return the following day for the closing ceremonies and installation services. Anyway, our man had lost. It was all over – I thought.

About three weeks after the election, I received a phone call at my church office. It was Dr. Turner. The call was simple, brief and direct. I was instructed to come to a meeting of the General Board in Raleigh on the following week at the First Baptist Church in downtown Raleigh. I was told to arrive an hour earlier and he would meet with me prior to the meeting and that I should plan to stay the entire day. That was the end of the call and it was completely strange to me. What on earth did he want with me? Didn't he know I was supporting his opponent? What on earth was a General Board?

I set out on the appointed date for First Baptist Church in downtown Raleigh. These were pre-GPS days so I had to depend on a paper map and road signs. Somehow I missed Raleigh – the state capital – and ended up in Garner, NC. Several stops at gas stations and convenience stores resulted in my arriving at the First Baptist Church with my four-cylinder Dodge K Car (Carolina blue in color) tired from the sense of lostness that I had cruelly imposed on her. I finally found out how to get inside the mammoth building that stands in the shadow of the State Capitol (or maybe the State Capitol stands in First Baptist's shadow). I asked for Dr. Turner and I was shown to the Church's Library where I found Dr. Turner pacing the floor.

He lit into me as a supervisor on a loading dock would light into a rookie who was late for his first day. Well over six feet tall, this massive man towered over me and bent his regal frame toward my face and peppered me with questions. I finally got a chance to answer him and explained that I was late because I had gotten lost and ended up in Garner. He stopped talking and this bewildered look came to his face. I would later discover that he told Queen Esther Blackwell, a member of my congregation, that if I was too dumb to find the city of Raleigh, I was surely too dumb to be of any help to the Kingdom of God. At this point, I would not have disputed that claim. When his look of bewilderment (or sheer disgust) was passed, he told me that one of his priorities in the presidency would be to bring young pastors into the work and functioning of the convention. He had opened up several seats on the Convention's General Board – its chief policymaking group – and he wanted to fill those seats with me and other young preachers. He told me that I wasn't expected to do much or to talk much. My main job would be to listen and learn. He also asked me if I could spell. I thought that was a weird question and I sought to impress him with the factoid that I had a degree in English. He was not impressed, but went on to tell me that he would have me appointed Assistant Recording Secretary of the General Board. It may or may not happen at that first meeting, but just be ready whenever it happened. It did indeed happen at that first meeting and I learned that E. B. Turner usually got whatever it was that E. B. Turner wanted. When the pronouncements from the oracle called Turner was done, he left the room and I found my way into my first General Board meeting.

If I was out of place in the counting room during the election at White Rock, I was even more out of place in the General Board meeting. It was a war zone. The verbal sparring, the parliamentary outmaneuvering of one side over another and the outright discourtesy to each other was something I was not accustomed to hearing among preachers. "Point of order" was the war cry of the day. It was not unusual for several people to claim the floor at the same time. President Turner was not at all timid in telling whatever speaker who was on the floor that they were out of order simply because he did not like what they were saying. At one point, he simply told the pastor of the church in which we were meeting to "sit down and shut up!" I didn't know what I was in, but I was sure that I wanted to get out.

Here is the amazing thing: after hours of confrontation, argument and next to name calling, the meeting adjourned and the men who were about to knock each other out were planning to go to a local buffet for lunch. It was as if the meeting had not really occurred. The conversation changed from antagonistic disagreement to cheerful banter. Dr. Turner asked if I wanted to come along, but I declined. I was too bewildered by what I had just seen and I was too broke to spend gas money eating with my new Board mates. I told him that I was headed home and he said to expect his call in a couple of weeks. He called as he said and, this time, summoned me to Lumberton. It would be the first of many, many calls at odd hours of the day or night summoning me to appear hither, thither or yon. Other than having to preach a funeral in my own congregation, I was expected to drop whatever I was doing at a moment's notice and meet him at this place or that. I often grumbled, but I never complained. Looking back, I know what he was doing.

I later found out that my member, Queen Esther Blackwell, had been a college classmate of Dr Turner and she literally knew everyone who was anyone in state convention life. She knew Dr. Humphrey as well. She had told both of them about her new young pastor and called in favors from years ago that, without regard to whoever won the election, I would be mentored by the state convention president. "Queenie" (as everyone affectionately called her) saw some potential in me and she wanted this diamond in the rough to be polished by the best in North Carolina Baptist life. A deal, unbeknownst to me, had been struck and it fell Dr. Turner's lot to fulfill the commitment.

E. B. Turner became far more than a ministerial mentor. He became a father figure. The more he got to know me, the more he liked me and the more I loved him. In time, he would take to telling people that I was the son he never had, but that was always behind my back. In my presence, he would teasingly (and lovingly) introduce me as his wife's favorite son. His modus operandi was simple: he was going to immerse me deeply in the pool of Baptist life in North Carolina and he would not let me come up for air until I had yielded to these Baptist influences. He did a good job in making me love Baptist life and commit to a lifelong dedication to missions and to cooperation among churches.

Dr. Turner was not a "Baptist best" kind of man. He was a "Baptist first" guy. He did not believe that the Baptist was the only way to express our Christian stewardship and commitment. He had good friends in so many denominations and preached (and cooperated) across racial and denominational lines. He just felt that Baptists ought neither to be ashamed of their heritage and legacy and should be their denomination and its objectives first in devotion and commitment.

I cannot count the number of trips I made to his church and home in Lumberton. The meetings that he summoned me to attend are almost as countless as the sands on the beach. Anything he was on or in or even vaguely connected to would sooner or later be graced by my presence. The instructions that he gave to me were always the same: listen, observe and say not "nary a word". On the ride from this or that meeting, he and I would discuss what had happened, what his strategy was, what his next move would be and how he would win a concession. One needs to only travel to Lumberton – the hub of his ministry for more than fifty years – to see how he positively impacted that community and the lives of the people who lived in that community.

We traveled together often and he was always the driver and the conversation starter. I sometimes thought that the conversation was more often to keep him awake on some long road back to Lumberton. But a chance to talk to him was always my delight. I quickly came to appreciate what a great man he was and how fortunate I was to have been taken under his wing.

When he retired to his native home following his pastoral service in Lumberton, I was delighted on two fronts: first, I had become the executive head of the convention that he had served as president and, secondly, he and Mrs. Turner were closer to me in Goldston, NC than they had been to me in Lumberton, NC. His health began to fail after retirement and he was soon not able to drive. I bought a very large and very expensive automobile for the express purpose of being able to drive him around in his declining years as he had done in my early days. I was his chauffeur only twice before he went to live in that house not made with hands.

On one of those two trips in the car bought expressly for his comfort, he asked me a question out of the blue. I did not see it coming. He asked if I appreciated him. I assured him that I did. A few minutes later, he asked the same thing. I bore down on the assurance that I appreciated him so. Just before we reached his house, he posed the same question again. I was growing somewhat frustrated and bewildered as to why he kept coming to the same question that he obviously knew the answer. I was unyielding in my praise and gratitude for him and we sat for some minutes in the driveway of his home. For perhaps the only time in our time together, he was letting me do the talking. I ended my talk by telling him that I owed him more than I could ever repay. After a few moments of silence, he said to me that I could repay him by doing for some other young preacher what he had done for me over the years. I did not have to say anything to him. Somehow he knew I would take on that charge and I would be relentless about it.

I have tried to keep that unspoken promise over the years. I have sought to open the doors of opportunity for young preachers just as E. B. Turner opened so many doors for me. I have tried to mentor as I have mentored. I have worked at a fever pitch to make good on what he expected from me. Occasionally that expensive car I bought to be Dr. Turner's chariot in his declining years will seemingly turn its direction toward that sacred burial ground at the Roberts Chapel Baptist Church in Goldston, NC. Seemingly with a mind of its own, that car climbs the crest of a proud hill upon which Dr. and Mrs. Turner are buried, one beside the other. It seems that the vehicle automatically brings me to the solemn quiet and heavy calm of that hill crest where I will lean against the large granite stone with the prominent letter "T-U-R-N-E-R." There will I again commit to doing for others as he and she did for me. And with teary eyes and a grateful heart, I will ride in that vehicle that was never intended to be ridden in alone to the next assignment where I can tell our Baptist witness and promote our Baptist promise. Though I am in the car alone, I am not lonely. My passengers are the memories of years and years of instruction and inspiration from my mentors. Those memories are good company indeed.

J. W. Brown. Arthur R. White. E. Burns Turner. While their names may top a list of persons of influence in my life and ministry, they are by no means the complete list of the many people in my life who have had an impact on making me the minister and the person that I am. I energetically reject the concept of a "self-made person." I cannot fathom such an anomaly. People move in and out of our lives with the precision of a symphony being played by a well-rehearsed orchestra. Each instrument in an orchestra makes a contribution to the music that is being played, but every instrument is different in sound and in purpose. There are parts of the oratorio when some instruments play prominently and other times when they stand silent. Yet they all influence the tone and tenor of the piece that is being played.

I have been blessed by the rise and fall of the human instruments that God has sent in and out of the music that has been my life and ministry. From them I have learned so much. But even those of dubious reputation and questionable character have also been my teachers. From their examples, I have construed the boundaries of acceptability. I have learned from them what not to do. Whatever their contribution, I am grateful to have been their students – whether by Divine intention or by human accident.

The late Reverend Dr. Harold S. Diggs could pick apart an argument and a Scripture text with the precision of a neurosurgeon. He rarely lost an argument and he was seldom overcome by a text. He was a teacher. Robert F. Davis (not a preacher, but a deacon and a dear friend) taught me much by telling me old stories about his grandfather, the late Reverend Dr. Fisher R. Mason. In long rides back from revival services that I was preaching, Bobby Davis would tell me these stories that he remembered from his grandfather's ministry and they tinged my thoughts about my own ministry. He was my teacher. Freddie Davis ran the print operation at Averett College. In my brief sprint as his work-study student, he exposed me to the value of organizing my assignments, the importance of fulfilling commitments and the value of being on time. He was my teacher. The Reverend John B. Doe, Jr. was thirty years my senior when we first met after I assumed my maiden pastorate at Pelham. Only twenty years old at the time, I had very little to offer in terms of experience to be taken very seriously as a pastor or as a cleric. Rev. Doe befriended me and shared with me from the wealth of his experience. When he was elected Moderator of our local Baptist Association, it was to me that he turned to be his Vice Moderator and sidekick. He was my teacher. My aunt, Wanda Ellis, would spend hours with me as a child at our modest kitchen table showing me how to write in cursive. I imitated (though never mastered) her beautiful flowing penmanship, but that regular ritual did much to help me learn to appreciate that words were beautiful things. She was my teacher.

The preachers of my youth declared that God was prone to "make a way out of no way." My life has been touched with a myriad of way makers. If Dr. Gardner C. Taylor is the Dean of America's African-American preachers, then Dr. James Donald Ballard is North Carolina's preaching Dean. I crossed paths with Dr. Ballard many years ago as a result of his attending a funeral at which I was eulogist. Dr. Ballard claims that he was impressed with my delivery and, thereafter, began to open his esteemed pulpit to my preaching. Considering that I was a pastoral and preaching novice at the time that we met, it was indeed risky business for Dr. Ballard to so honor me. Fortunately, his reputation was so well established that even the poor preaching and directionless meanderings of a youthful preacher-pastor like me did not put a dent in the armor of the esteem he had built as a preacher-pastor. Yet he did welcome me as a junior colleague in the craft and the knowledge that I was good enough for J, D. Ballard's pulpit made the way for countless preaching opportunities across the years. One of my most treasured possessions in life is a friendship with Dr. Ballard that spans almost thirty years. Now in retirement from a distinguished career as pastor of the United Metropolitan Missionary Baptist Church of Winston-Salem, North Carolina, he spends his days serving as interim pastor to extremely fortunate congregations across North Carolina. From time to time, he will call upon me to preach in his stead in one of his interim assignments. On those very fortunate occurrences for me, I always introduce myself as "the only preacher in America who is crazy enough to show up in J. D. Ballard's place." While that always brings a chuckle to the people gathered who were expecting to hear Dr. Ballard, but who have to make themselves content with me, I know that I am not now nor will I ever be in his preaching class. I do nothing to add value to his reputation, but his recommendation of my ministry across the years has added great value to my name and reputation. I am grateful that he has been an instrument of God making ways for me.

I suspect that I may have overstated my case as it relates to the importance of mentorship. I have purposely been repetitive in hopes that, hearing this over and over, will cause it to be carved upon the hearts of young preachers: you need a good mentor as much as a great fish needs the oceans and the birds need to see the clouds. But I think it is critically important that young ministers have credible mentorship. Any example will not do. The young minister needs to hitch his/her wagon of service to the mightiest preaching horses available. For when that young minister becomes mired in the muck and mire that is a part of ministry in the twenty-first century, only the strength and strong counsel of strong mentors will pull that preaching wagon through the mud to solid ground. I believe strongly in being mentored.

Likewise, I think it is the obligation of the senior minister to offer mentorship to the younger ones. Those of us who have found our way successfully through the thicket of Christian ministry should stand as signs pointing the younger ones that follow up to the "more excellent way." It is not that young people in ministry will not make errors. They will. Some will be egregious and some will threaten the core and effectiveness of the ministry to which they have been called. But if the old souls will take some interest in the development of the tender hearts and minds of those who are in the dawn of their careers, the young will make fewer mistakes, in general, and few career-ending mistakes, specifically. Anything other than this is a missed opportunity to achieve greatness, on the part of the spiritual mentee, and a missed duty to help mold greatness on the part of the mentor.

"Lessons for Ministry"

1. If you are young in ministry, seek a good mentor. If you are in the practice of ministry, seek out friends who can allow you to learn from their experiences and expertise. If you are in the dusk of your ministry, find a young person whom you can mentor. Such is the natural order of things.

2. You will likely have more than one mentor in your ministry. God sends persons who have the skills that you need for the particular place and time that you are in your own ministry. Their strengths are the strengths that God needs you to develop for your present or for your future service. Follow those mentors closely and gain as much as you can from the brief time that they will intersect with the road you are traveling.

3. Appreciate and honor the mentors and teachers who come to walk alongside you on your journey. My great regret is that I may have failed in letting the people that God sent to teach me know of their value to me. I often realized that too late. Do not be haunted with that regret. Tell those persons whose light guides you as the North Star guides the captain of a ship on a midnight sea that they have lit a candle in your life and that candlelight has chased the darkness of doubt, fear and ignorance away.

CHAPTER 9

"BETTER MIND. OH SISTER, HOW YOU WALK ON THE CROSS"

A STANZA FROM AN old prayer meeting song sung in African-American congregations in the south begins *"Better mind, O Sister, how you walk on the cross ... your foot may slip and your soul be lost."* Beyond the people and experiences that have colored my outlook on life and my perspective on ministry, there have been other influences that have put shape to my character and undergirded my belief system. Some of these influences have been overt while others have been subtle. I bring them to the discussion because I am so aware of their influence. Had they not been managed properly, my foot could have easily slipped and my life's focus could have been entirely different. Ranking very high among those influences are race and social justice.

I was born in the rich farmland of Southampton County, Virginia. The flat land of Tidewater married a temperate climate which was an ideal circumstance for farming. Peanuts were a staple of the community in which I was born, but other crops were plentiful. Whatever grew well in the soil and would produce a good cash return at harvest was what we grew. Farms had provided the source of substantial wealth for some Southamptonians, but none of the then barons of wealth were of a darker hue. Slavery had produced the wealth that several of the prominent white families now enjoyed. However, it was considered impolite to discuss exactly how those families enjoyed their high standard of living. The unspoken truth was that African-American laborers – first as slaves, then as sharecroppers, and finally as low paid workers on white-owned farms – had been the source of the privilege and power enjoyed by a few in the little town of Capron, Virginia.

As a child, most of my interactions with people was within the confines of our African-American spaces in our community: homes, churches, gathering places. My few ventures outside the safety of these communities was an unusual world for me. A visit to the Main Street bank was rare, an occasional trip to the local post office, a brief stop at a business owned by whites but frequented by blacks was the extent of my interracial interaction. For most of my youth, I would be driven down Main Street – which was completely white majority owned – on the way to "The Store" or to our church. It was simply an experience of passing through. I had very little interest in what was going on there and my family had very little business to conduct there. The main thoroughfare of our sleepy little village was not a place where black people spent much time or congregated. It was a place only to pass through. Because our "black" world was so full of life, it didn't bother me very much as a child that these tall, but invisible walls separated our community by race and class and status.

I have previously mentioned that I was sickly as a child and had some severe episodes of asthma. My grandmother would take me to the county seat – the town of Courtland – to see a doctor. I do not know if this was because there was no doctor in our little town, or if there was a doctor, he did not see African-American patients, or if it was because the public assistance that my family received dictated the trek to the county seat for our medical care. The memorable impression of a visit to Dr. Daughtry's office was the clear impression that there was a difference between the races. The doctor's office had a single front entrance which opened into a long room which was divided by a wall down the center of the room. There was no sentinel at the entrance, but the visitors to Dr. Daughtry instinctively knew what to do: White people turned to the left and found space on "their" side of the waiting room while African-American patients turned to the right and found a place on "their" side of the waiting room. I do not know if a sign was posted or not. All I knew is that after entering the common entrance, my grandmother would clasp my hand tighter and lead me to "our" side. As a child, I always paused to glimpse on both entering and exiting the building to see how the "other" side looked.

Our side was poorly lit with only hardback chairs along one wall. There was scarcely any reading material there save for a few outdated magazines, most with their covers in poor condition. I remember nothing adorning its sterile white walls and its cold tile floors were nondescript. "Their" side was completely different as I ascertained after numerous entering glances and parting peeks. Artwork graced the walls, a comfortable looking rug covered the tile floor and the seating was all padded and newer. There were books and magazines which seemed to delight the white children who always seemed to be visiting a children's library instead of a doctor's office. No matter when I arrived, I never got to see the doctor until everyone on the other side of the wall had come and gone. This made for very long and sometimes miserable waits in the doctor's office.

Two separate doors led from the waiting room into the doctor's office in which a large wooden desk was the central and focal point of the large room. Like in the waiting space, there were chairs. But in his inner sanctum, there were only two chairs – one on either side of the desk. Depending upon which door had brought you into this space, you sat on either the right or the left side of the doctor's desk. Like in the waiting room, whites on the left side of the desk and African-Americans on the right side of the desk. When I was small enough to be held in my grandmother's lap, she sat in the chair on the right side with me in her arms. When I became big enough to command the seat for myself, she stood during the entire visit. Even though it was only the three of us in this private space – my grandmother, Dr. Daughtry and I, she dared not sit in the chair on the left and she was never invited to do so. That seat was not for black folks.

I did not understand all the intricacies of race at that time in my young life, but I did know that it simply did not seem fair for a white kid with a runny nose who arrived after my arrival at the doctor to get to see him before I did. That child had only to endure sniffles while my chest heaved and my breath was shallow from an attack of asthma. It did not seem right, nor just, nor Christian. But it just was ... it was the way things were done. I could not help but hide those things and my feelings in my heart. I still attended a segregated school and a not integrated Church. Equity and sameness among people was the norm. In this doctor's office, people were clearly being treated differently and, although I could not understand exactly why, I knew I did not like that.

Though the United States Supreme Court in the famed Brown v. Board of Education decision determined that separate public schools segregated by race was unconstitutional in 1954, word apparently did not reach us in Southampton County, Virginia until the early 1970's. The edicts coming from Washington and other parts of the nation did little to affect our community nor did they effect significant change. When the schools integrated in Southampton County, a trend familiar throughout the south was invoked. The former black high school became the junior high school where the former black high school principal would now be principal of the junior high school. Likewise and conversely, the former white high school became "the" high school with the executive leadership of the school remaining virtually unchanged. High school became a familiar place for the white children in our county, but it was a strange and threatening place for the African-American students who were now attending a school that we previously only passed by on our way to our black school.

Because the schools integrated when I was in junior high school, the transition to high school was somewhat easier. At least my classmates and I had a couple years' advantage of having white teachers and being in integrated classes. White children from families with money had the option of attending the all-white private academy in Courtland – less than two miles from the segregated offices of Dr. Daughtry. I understand that there was no "official" rule against African-American students being admitted to the Academy, but a strange guard whose name was "tuition" kept children of color from crossing the threshold of the front door.

I do not recall explosive tension in high school because the classes that came before me bore the brunt of the discord between the races. By the time of my arrival in tenth grade, it had been indoctrinated in the psyche of most of the African-American youth that the "system" was not designed to work in our favor. As a result, we were told that we had to be better than good in order to succeed. If we were athletes, we were expected to be super athletes. If we were studious, we had to claim a permanent pace on the honor roll. To get ahead, we had been told, we had to be more than good sometime, we had to be great all of the time. Our white counterparts, we had been warned, were automatically put into a favored status. To compete, we would have to think harder, work harder and study harder. With that heavy pronouncement on my life, I gravitated toward nine other young people whose parents had similarly instructed and indoctrinated them. Together we became an inseparable band of kindred spirits. We were eight young women and two young men who were uncommonly smart, high achievers and strictly disciplined teenagers. For the most part, we took the same academically gifted classes and joined the same extracurricular clubs. We lived all across the county so our paths rarely crossed on the weekends, but we were inseparable on Mondays through Fridays. When we could all find rides to the football or basketball games, we would be joined at the hips it seems.

Although the "gang of ten" came from very different socio-economic backgrounds, we found commonality in our mutual ability to sense injustice and do what we could to stamp it out. It was as if we all had antennae which were highly sensitive to the plight of other students who were being treated unfairly or who, due to race, were being disadvantaged by some policy of the school. We thought it our sacred duty to bring it to someone's attention and, if the responsible adults would do nothing about it, take some action ourselves. We circulated numerous petitions demanding this, that or the other. We made numerous appointments with the principal to take up this cause or the other. The school's bulletin board was regularly posted with our hand lettered discussion starters: "Why are there no black students in physics class?" or "why are there no black athletic trainers for our nearly all-black football team?" or "why American history excluded black and native American history?" We were more in league with Martin Luther King, Jr. than we were with Malcolm X, but there were times when the tension in the air was a direct result of our feelings that black students were being treated unfairly. I suspect that we may have seen racism hiding beyond more bushes than were actually there, but it was a fact that we lived in a context where expectations for us as African-American youth were much lower than the expectations for our white counterparts. A case in point involves a visit to my high school guidance office that set the path that led me to college in Southwest Virginia.

In my sophomore year in high school, I began to seriously think about what I would do after graduation. I was torn between staying in Southampton County and pursuing my life as a minister and going to college to pursue another career. Mind you that I had no concept of full-time, professional ministry. It would be one or other as far as I knew. A few of the "gang of ten" had parents or other close relatives who had been college educated and it became clear that most of my little gang would be going off to college. But I had no clue where to start or where to go or how to prepare. Not wanting my friends to know that I was clueless, I went by the office next door to the principal's office with GUIDANCE prominently displayed in bold letters. Guidance was exactly what I needed and letters that bold had to indicate that this commodity was in good supply.

I had been sent to the guidance office many times before, but never on a college choosing adventure. My trips to see the counselor were usually a compromise by some teacher choosing to banish me to the counselor's office rather than to the principal's office for some protest that I had staged or planned. It had become rather routine and I had come to know the African-American guidance counselor quite well. (Secretly I was encouraged by the African-American counselor to continue my fights for justice as I saw it even though it was probably seen by the white faculty as proper punishment for a smart, black kid with way too much Martin Luther King, Jr. in him.) On the day in question, the African-American counselor that I normally saw was out sick. I had to see the white counselor for the first time.

I quickly and proudly announced to her as soon as the door to her office was closed that I was there for guidance in choosing what college to attend. She looked surprised as she almost fell into her seat. As she sat, the broad smile on her face that had been the dam holding back her laughter burst. She very audibly laughed at my suggestion. She promptly went on to tell me that she knew about my family's background (apparently my frequent trips to her colleague's office had sparked an interest in who this little militant youth was) and did not think I was college material. She began to pepper me with questions that I had come to her to discover the answers. How would I pay for it? What did I want to study? Where would I go to college? Public or private? Large campus or small college town? I knew absolutely nothing, but I was totally put off and offended by her attitude. Her guidance that day amounted to suggesting that I continue to do well in my studies and when I graduated try to get a job in the Tidewater shipbuilding trade and I would make a good living for myself.

I was not hurt or humiliated. I was mad. I was determined that she would know that I was more determined than ever to go to somebody's college somewhere, somehow. Her attitude had sealed my fate. When she asked for what seemed to be the umpteenth time what school I wanted to attend, I noticed that she had arranged the college catalogs on the edge of her desk along the wall in alphabetical order. The first one was Averett College. I had never heard of Averett before and she was terribly tickled when I announced that I wanted to go to Averett. It was funny to her that I mispronounced the name (giving the first syllable a short "a" sound as opposed to a long "a" sound.) She proceeded to inform me that Averett was definitely out of my family's reach. As a private college, the tuition was very high and there would be no way our family could afford to send me to a private school. She re-visited her earlier suggestion about a job in the shipbuilding trades and, maybe if I just insisted on a higher education, a few courses at the local community college. I heard very little of what she was saying. Instead of listening to her, I was practicing over and over in my head the correct pronunciation of Averett. My heart was fixed and my mind was made up.

I did gain admission to Averett College. In the late 1970's, Averett had an early admission program. Under this program, high school juniors who showed promise and good grades could win college acceptance in their junior year of high school. I applied and was admitted. I had great delight in rushing into the guidance office at high school on the day after my acceptance letter came. I could not wait to tell the laughing counselor that I would definitely not be going into the shipbuilding trade unless, of course, I was going into management there after getting my degree from Averett College. There was very little amusement from her on that day as neither she nor her reading glasses could believe the words that danced off a sheet of Averett College admissions office letterhead.

I was sad that my other nine buddies had chosen to go to other colleges. Most of them settled in the Richmond, Virginia area for their college experiences. One went to Norfolk and the other male in the posse chose Charlottesville, Virginia. Our high school graduations were our commencement into new lives where we would rarely ever intersect over the coming years. I owe much to their friendship and to the mutual support that we gave to each other. They were my cohorts in justice and we brainstormed over how we would make things better for African-American students at our high school all while enjoying the wide eyed optimism of being a couple years shy from the twenty-somethings.

My grandmother paid a neighbor to load his pickup truck with my footlocker that contained the totality of my worldly possessions. The three of us jammed into the cab of the truck and off we went in a westward direction to take me to a place I would make home. The trip from Capron to Danville is a two-and-a-half-hour trip of around 135 miles. Having never traveled west before, I thought it to be as far as Chicago or California. It had not really occurred to me that I would live on my own for the first time in my life. That reality began to settle in on me during the ride. As the flatland of Tidewater began to transform into the rolling hills of the Piedmont, I had an eerie feeling that things would never be the same for me.

We arrived in the city and quickly found the Averett campus. My footlocker and I were ejected at the corner of West Main Street and Woodland Drive. For some strange reason, there was a postal service mail box on this corner. I took strange comfort in the ridiculous idea that if things did not work out for me, I could mail myself back home.

My grandmother and her hired driver were anxious to get back to the security of familiar surroundings before dark so they did not wait for me to find where to go or what to do. I kissed and hugged my grandmother and she left. She would not return until three years later when I marched across the stage as a college graduate.

I somehow discovered the way to Bishop Dormitory where I would live for the next three years. Exactly how I managed to drag that footlocker up the three flights of stairs to my floor in Bishop Hall without the assistance of wheels, the convenience of an elevator or the kindness of a friend, I will never know. I was most likely being driven completely on adrenalin at this point. I found Room 21 on the third floor of Bishop Hall with great delight. I opened the door to a brand new life.

During the summer, the college had sent letters informing all incoming freshmen of whom their roommate would be. We were encouraged to write to our soon to be roomie and get acquainted. My roommate and I exchanged one or two letters. We did not find out very much about each other except for the very basics: where we were from, what our majors were and the fact that we were from different races. He was white and I was black. Although this fact alarmed my family and circle of support at home, it did not disturb me at all. I was very open to the idea of expanding my appreciation for and understanding of other races and cultures. I somehow had convinced myself that white people in the rest of the world would be very different from the white people in my native place.

I opened the door to my first and only dorm room at Averett and discovered that my roommate had already arrived and had claimed over half of the dorm room space. It did not matter because I had so little that I really did not need the space he had left for me. I entered the room and stood for a moment admiringly gazing upon my roommate's shiny new things: stereo and speakers, guitar, piles of clothes (some with the tags still on) and posters on the wall, books on the desk and shoes sticking out from under his bed. When I turned to look at my yet barren part of the room, I was quickly and unpleasantly made aware that my side was not quite as empty as I had thought. It seems that my new roommate had left me a welcome gift. There, atop the chest of drawers which would be my primary private space for the next three years, was a watermelon with a note taped to it. The note read, "Welcome! Something to make you feel at home."

I was incensed, furious and madder than (as we were want to say at home) a wet hen! I had not felt this kind of emotion since the day, two years prior, that the high school guidance counselor had made fun at my desire to go to college. I never learned if the act by my roommate was out of pure racism or if it was some insensitive joke that my new roomie thought would be funny. It really did not matter at the moment. I raised the window to my third floor dorm room and threw the watermelon out. It splattered over the concrete sidewalk and neatly manicured lawn beneath my window. I stood at the window – red-faced with anger – and watched shocked faces look up to see from where mobile fruit had been launched. It did not take long for word to travel around our tiny college campus that there is a crazy dude on the top floor of Bishop Hall. Perhaps my new roommate heard about the incident or perhaps he even saw it. I never knew. He did not come into the room until late in the night. I had organized my things and was laying fully dressed across my bed. I was prepared for either flight or fight. He eased in the doorway. Upon entry, he fell into the traction beam of a stare that went right through him much like the "phasers on stun" that I had seen a thousand times on the television show "Star Trek." He quietly said, "Hey, man." I said nothing as I was still too angry to utter a word. I just rose, left the room and intentionally slammed the door as loudly as I thought humanly possible.

On the ground floor of our building was the student center, student post office boxes, a small snack bar and several seating areas for students to hang out to play cards, pool or foosball. To control my anger and minimize my rage, I instinctively began to clean up the student center. My grandmother had kept a spotless and immaculate house and it took many years for me to break the housekeeping habit. I started by throwing away paper and discarded cups and cans. I ended with a frantic arranging and re-arranging then arranging again the student center furniture. Apparently the word spread that the watermelon tossing crazy dude in Bishop Hall has taken to unapproved custodial duties in the student center. A woman who would become my best friend at college and "sister" in life rushed over from Fugate Hall to meet me. She invited me to the safety and security of a basement suite of African-American female students. That basement suite would become my refuge for the next three years. It was a place where I would have family and nurture whenever I needed either of them. A knock on the fire exit on the side of the building would bring some suite mate scurrying to open the fire exit and usher some African-American student into the safe place that was Suite 101. Dorm rules and visitation hours be damned! A knock on the fire exit door of Fugate Hall meant that some black student needed an escape from a cold or hostile world. That door would open at any time of the day or night and become the place to vent and learn how to "sing the Lord's song in a strange land."

Needless to say, my first roommate moved out without saying a word to me by the end of our second week together. Apparently my fame had spread so that no other white student wanted to be a part of the college's social experiment in providing a diverse cultural experience for the residents of Room 21 in Bishop Hall. I remained without a roommate for the remainder of my first semester in college.

One might think that the experiences of my youth, of high school and of college as it relates to race would have negatively colored my outlook on people who are different from me. Nothing could be farther from the truth. The Averett experience was invaluable in getting me to understand other people's culture, values, norms, mores and religions. The college was a community richer in diversity than anything I had known or experienced before. Somehow I embraced it all and wanted so much to experience everything that my microcosm of the world could bring to me.

So I made friends easily with anyone who showed themselves friendly. I made friends in great numbers. My circle of friends was large and, unlike the "gang of ten" from high school, my college friends and I had very little in common. There was G – a Cuban woman with the most profane mouth that I had ever heard. B – the first African-American openly gay male I had ever met – was a part of the circle. I remember T – the campus jock whose sexual exploits included women on, off and all around the campus. I befriended M – a nerdy little guy from Southwest Virginia who was afraid of everything and everyone including loud noise and silent nights. One of my best buddies was K – a white woman from western Virginia who had only seen a handful of black people in her entire life and whose father was a card-carrying racist. Her delight was being able to touch and style my afro. There was S – a beautiful African-American woman who could out-drink, out-smoke and out-curse any merchant marine, foreign or domestic. I can't ever forget P – a Pentecostal young man who spent half of every day praising God and the other half of every day fighting Satan. I made friends with R – a woman from New York City who knew more of the ways of the world than I ever knew existed from the hamlet of Capron. My friends were male and female, black and white, straight and gay, liberal and conservative, outlandish and straight-laced. Some of them drank and smoked, while I prayed and worried about them. But their shortcomings and their honesty with me made me love each of them all the more. I have never exactly figured out what attracted me to this very eclectic group of citizens of the world nor did I know what drew them to me. But over the course of my college career, these were the people who supported me and whom I supported, the people who shared life's joys and sorrows, and the people who always had my back. All of my friends where not friends with all my other friends. Not everyone in my circle was as welcoming as I was. But I spread affection for people broadly and deeply. Their friendship made me happy.

It might be true that I discovered the depth and absolute necessity of the love of God when I was in college among this odd group of people. It's easy to love the people who are like you are, who share your interests, who come from where you come from and who do not challenge your ideas or values. It is quite another thing to love someone who is different. To learn to love others just as you love yourself also opens up the possibility that you will learn to love yourself as God loves you: completely, without reservation and without boundaries.

I suspect on some other level that we each needed each other and each other's validation. All of us were flawed in some very obvious way. None of us were the ideal candidate for a private school education. I was poor, black and had come to college from what seemed to be a trip across a galaxy from where I had started. Each of my friends, in their own way, was branded a castaway in one way or another. What I learned was that it is pointless to point fingers when the people at whom you are pointing are on the same raft as you. Because of this colorful group of characters who formed the inner circle of my most trusted confidants and advisors and fellow strugglers, I learned some very important things: first, all people are flawed and, second, the best people are sometimes those with the deepest flaws and, finally, all people deserved to be loved and respected.

It was at Averett that I began to seriously struggle with the religious concept of "loving the sinner while hating the sin." Prior to my coming to college, my spiritual context was very certain about what was right and what was wrong. It was as if all of life had been catalogued in two columns: right and wrong. All that one needed to do was run a finger down the list until arriving at the particular deed in question. Whatever list it was on, certified its wholesomeness. My faith community had taken all responsibility for my thinking through ethics and values and choice. I was comfortable with the resolution that my faith community had set in stone. Then I came to college and kept encountering very good and faithful people whom my faith community would have labeled as sinners without thought or pause.

My problem with those who professed such a high level of righteousness and perfect judgment was that they often used the same language to describe the sinner as they did the sin. While they professed to be able to differentiate, they far too often saw them as one and the same. I was far from developing a complete Christology at this time of my young life, but I related much more to a loving, welcoming and forgiving Christ than I did with an angry, vengeful and punishing God. Averett was a Church-related school and the campus was teeming with young people with various religious identities. Some were on a search for God and truth while others were adamantly attempting to abandon every religious aspect of their personhood. Far too often, I encountered young people whose religious views made them intolerant, and self-absorbed and simply inhospitable. In such attitudes, I could not find Christ. But as I met more and more people who were very different from me and whose lifestyles and life choices were radically different from my own, I could not get away from the loving embrace that Rev. Lassiter had given to me on the night of my conversion. I felt that I needed to be as welcoming to others since Christ had been so welcoming to me.

This valuing of people who are different undergirded my years in the pastorate. I found it easy to identify with the "least of these" who found their way into the places where I was pastor. I would like to think that many of them changed their ways and sought "a more excellent way" in their personal lives. However, if that happened, it was due to their finding their own paths and traveling at their own pace. It had nothing to do with the condemnation, rejection and near harassment that they received from many corners of their lives. Fortunately, I was well grounded in my faith and values by the time that I arrived at college and the experimentation that most young adults was not so great a temptation to me. I am not suggesting that I was perfect in any manner because I was not. Like all youth, bright lights and fast lanes are intoxicating. All in all, I was only a moderate sinner and I was too afraid to stray too far off the beaten paths.

To have been called to ministry at so tender an age could have easily been an impetus for me to throw caution to the wind when I was in college. Having had such great expectations (and totally unrealizable expectations) thrust upon me when I was just fifteen, it is amazing that I did not major in doing things that neither God nor my grandmother would be pleased. From my own "rainbow coalition" of friends, I found both the encouragement and the opportunity to do all manner of things that would have made the folk back home sorely disappointed in me. Some I did (and enjoyed). Some I tried (and wasn't successful). Some simply did not interest me at all. But none of those things made Christ need me less for His purposes. I was wrapped in the grace of God, the love of Christ and I knew I had the sweet communion of the Holy Ghost. The love that my motley crew heaped on me only confirmed what I already knew about God's love for me.

However, because my focus was squarely on making a better life for me and to never bring shame on my family or friends, I also strongly believed that I had to hold the standard of being a minister above the muddy places of life. I did not ever want my example to be a barrier to someone else having a closer walk with God. So I learned the value of discretion. I sharpened the discernment of deciding what to tell and what to keep between myself and God. I began to shape a lifelong belief that doing is much lower on the ladder of righteousness than being is. If I can figure out what God wants me to be, I will know what I am supposed to do. I knew I was to be a vessel of God's love so I knew that what I had to do was love this unbelievable cast of characters. My friends never forgot that I was a preacher, but they never perceived me as holier than they were. They loved me enough to give me the space I needed to live out my faith just as I gave them space to be whomever they were at heart.

Race and class, racism and classism all contributed to my worldview. Undoubtedly I was impacted by the experiences that I had as a youth and young adult in my interactions with a majority white environment. Yet injustice and unfair treatment of people did not make me bitter; they made me better. Better in the sense that I was determined to overcome whatever obstacles were put before me because of my race or of my background or of my origins in the backwoods of southern Virginia. I did not strive to be better than my peers, but I did strive to always be better than the expectations that others had of me. In a cultural context as I found myself at Averett, this was a constant pursuit and an unyielding challenge. Browning was right when it seems that he spoke to me saying, *"A man's reach should exceed his grasp, Or what's a heaven for?"*

My experiences also made me better in the sense that I became an activist. To correct wrongs and to balance inequities was as much a part of my ministry to the world as was sharing the Gospel. I saw no disconnect between Jesus the Savior and Jesus the prophet or Jesus the right-er of wrongs. To follow Christ, I had decided, meant to stand for justice and to be on the side of the oppressed. To give voice to the voiceless became an integral part of who I am as a man and who I am as a minister.

I am from Southampton County, Virginia. Its hallowed soil was the birthplace of persons who saw justice, freedom and equality as the birthrights of all people and not of just the privileged. Dred Scott was born in Southampton County. Born in 1795, Dred Scott sued for freedom as a slave and his case was ultimately heard by the United States Supreme Court in the *Dred Scott v Sanford* case. In 1857, the court erred and decided that no African-American could claim American citizenship as slaves and, therefore, had no standing to sue for a right of freedom. Anthony William Gardiner was born in Southampton County in 1820. He and his family moved to Liberia under the graces of the American Colonization Society in 1831. The Society was founded to aid the return of African-Americans to Africa. It founded the colony of Liberia and Anthony W. Gardiner became Liberia's ninth president. John Brown was born enslaved in Southampton County. Following the Civil War, Brown was elected to represent the County in the 1867-68 Convention to re-write the state's constitution. Defeating two whites to win election to the Convention, Brown won nearly 98% of the African-American vote to win a seat at the Convention. And Nat Turner was born in Southampton County.

I am still puzzled and angry that I knew so little of Nat Turner when growing up as a boy in Southampton County. He was never mentioned in our history books nor in our classes. His name was recalled from time to time, but only with derision by whites and in whispers by blacks. It was during my time at Averett that my own research brought me to understand that much of my youthful life had been spent on much of the same ground where events of the 1831 rebellion had taken place. When I learned that the rebellion that Turner led had occurred on August 21, 1831 and my conversion had happened on August 21 one hundred thirty-eight years later, I was awestruck. To me, this coincidence had to have some great, cosmic meaning for my life and I became nearly obsessed about learning as much about Nat Turner as I could.

There were striking parallels: he was a preacher; I was a preacher. He learned to read and write at a young age; I fell in love with reading and writing when young. We were both born in the same County though more than one hundred years separated our births. I was so impressed with Turner's fight for freedom and I felt some strange connection. When others criticized his methods as nothing more than a murderous rampage, I saw it no differently than the bloody wars of the American Revolution and the American Civil War where many died for the cause of freedom. When others saw Nat Turner as a tragic figure, I saw him in a heroic light. Years after leaving college, I took some inspiration from his understanding of the imprint of God upon his life to be obedient to God despite the risk and without measuring the sacrifice required. While I have never been confronted with the unction to take up arms, I have – for the better part of my life – known that sometimes (and for some things) one just has to fight.

Lessons for Ministry:

1. There are experiences and circumstances in your life that can shape you for ministry and service. God called you knowing full well who you are, where you come from, and the circumstances surrounding your upbringing. None of these factors are beyond the reach of God's use. Be open to exploring how your past can influence your present and your future.

2. God is not limited to using only the favored and the plentiful in one's life to His greater glory. God can also use the pain and the defeats of your own life to bring light and life to others. Be open to the possibility of your circumstances have uniquely

positioned you to be used by God in a certain way. Pray that you will discover God's leadings and His pleadings for you.

3. Your options for dealing with disadvantages are only two: these can make you bitter or these can make you better. Unfortunately, ministry is not an even road. It is bumpy and it gets rough. Yet it is all yet under the authority and purpose of God. Pray for God's help in using life's bitters to help you make something better for someone else in the world.

4. People have flaws. So do you. However, flaws do not restrict the rivers of love that flow from the heart of God and they should not prevent ministers from loving others despite their flaws. A good preacher friend, Dr. Donaldson Jones, has a brilliant take on John 3:16. We normally approach this passage from a soteriological perspective. It is about God's saving work through Christ. But Jones has suggested to me that it may be a model for ministry. If God's love is as comprehensive as John 3:16 suggests, then ministers are obligated to model that kind of love for people. We should love the world enough to give what God gave: He gave Himself. To a world marred by and mired in sin, He gave Himself. As ministers, we should give something of ourselves to those who come into our ministries. It is both what God expects and what God requires.

CHAPTER 10

"THERE'S A STILL, SMALL VOICE SAYING TO ME"

I ABANDONED MY FAMILY; my family did not abandon me. I am uncertain if that is the best way to begin this chapter, but it is sometimes easier to work your way through a difficult thing by doing the hardest part first. I am not exactly sure why this happened nor do I know exactly what all the contributing factors for this separation were. I do know this: from my earliest childhood memories, I always felt out of place at home. I was raised by a wonderful grandmother. I had a safe home life. I was happy as a child. All my needs and a good number of my wants were provided. For some reason, I always felt like I was a stranger among my own people. When I left home at eighteen to start college, I intrinsically knew that this was the beginning of a permanent separation from my kinsfolk. I remain troubled by the fact that I was not especially moved about it either way: I was not overcome with sadness and melancholy and I was not joyous and celebrative at it either. It had the air of inevitably about it, much like it was something akin to my destiny.

The physical estrangement started when I was in college. Having found myself in a strange and very different environment at college, I was propelled to declare my independence. I had been a rural dweller all of my eighteen years. Summer visits to the city were commonplace, but they always had the air of being temporary arrangements and not permanent placement. Alone and on my own for the first time created a near crisis moment for me. Since I was physically detached from the only family that I ever knew, I needed something to fill that void. Church helped some, but I needed to feel that somebody had my back. It was in college that I began a lifelong habit of befriending people and, in time, treating them like family. The more involved I became with my "new" family, the less I missed or needed my natural family. It was a gradual process that took years to fully achieve. However, when I returned to Capron, Virginia in 2002 to bury my grandmother, I knew that the breach was complete. With her death, the cord that kept me connected to my home place broke.

It is not true that my family did not reach out to me while I was in college. I knew that they were all very proud of me and that they were rooting for my success. After my grandmother's death and during the bittersweet process of going through a departed relative's things, I found a treasure trove of letters that I had sent home over the years. I was surprised that she had kept them all – neatly folded into their original envelopes, organized by the date of the postmark. Their age was belied by the inexpensive paper tinged with the yellowing that time brings to old papers. She was the principal person in my family with whom I stayed in touch and, with her death, the last and tender link to my family broke.

Money prevented me from going home very often when I started college. My family did not have the resources to send me "get home" money and I needed everything that I could earn to take care of myself while in college. I used a part of my meager earnings to send money home to my grandmother from time to time to fix something that had broken or to replace something that had worn out. In my mind, her comfort at home was much more important than seeing me during a holiday break. I convinced myself that I could do without a good helping of chicken and dumplings and that the sometimes sterile college cafeteria food would be just fine. For most of the times that the campus was closed for breaks, I persuaded the Dean of Residence Life to let me remain in the dorms. I always had one (and sometimes two) work study jobs on campus so it was not hard to get some college administrator to support my pleas to the Residence Life office. I needed a place to stay and they needed to get even more work out of me. It turned out to be a mutually beneficial arrangement. Over the three years that I was in college, I recall only one Christmas spent at home. The other two years were spent in Room 21 Bishop Hall with an always badly deformed Christmas tree that no one else would buy that the tree salesman was glad to get off his lot for a couple dollars. My "new" family would decorate the tree with all manner of things not Christmas (and often not at all religious). These "brothers and sisters" would gather often in my dorm room (usually to the chagrin of my poor roommate) to celebrate the coming Christmas. As I saw all of them off to visit family for the holiday, I would be left with the pitiful deformed tree and to anxiously awaiting their return after the holidays.

A high school classmate who was also from Capron was a part of the freshman class that joined the Averett student body when I did. She had a vintage Volkswagen bug and offered to haul me back and forth when she went home to visit her parents. This arrangement dissolved in short order as she went home less often and the "novelty" of a young black man taking long road trips with a young white girl made both her parents and my family at home uncomfortable. If it was during my college days that the physical separation from my family began, the emotional bonds began to fray much sooner.

I come from an eclectic group of people. My family is a small circle of people who always seemed to have something going on. Many times it was something to celebrate and occasionally it was something not to be mentioned in mixed company. We tended to be more on the loud side of things than the quiet and reflective sort. When we were together as a unit, we could be a bit overpowering upon meeting us for the first time. But we were always "laugh out loud" funny. If there is any certain gift that my family passed on to me genetically, it was an indefatigable sense of humor. Whenever anyone associated with our family was around, someone would be rolling over with laughter. Not only were we naturally funny people, we all seemed to have this almost supernatural ability to see humor in almost everything else in life. When it came to searching out the hilarity in the world, we all had x-ray vision. We could find something to laugh at in a funeral as easily as we did while watching a television sitcom. I do not know if this levity was a gift or a guise to mask unspoken pain. At times in my life, my sense of humor has served those dual roles.

No one was better at sarcasm or seeing humor peeking out from behind every aspect of life than my mother, Doris Marie Freeman. I think I fine-tuned my own sense of humor during the summers when she and other Philadelphia relatives would invade Capron for the annual summer visit down south. These annual times were the best times of my young life. They would be marked with card playing, drinking (some drinks were soft and others not so much), good eating and lots and lots of laughing. We were a rowdy crowd in a lot of ways. If your image of a family reunion is cramming the first four pews of the home church on Sunday morning, our family gatherings might well be wholly unfamiliar to you. What would be more on point is the image of a phonograph placed in the front stoop spinning Motown favorites while barefoot aunts and nephews, uncles and nieces, cousins and cousins taught each other the latest dance moves. That would have been our preferred Sunday devotional while our well-dressed neighbors passed on their way to church. I am surprised that our family did not somehow become owners of a chain of comedy clubs or boxing gyms. We excelled at both comedy and fighting. Fortunately, we laughed a lot more than we fought.

Crude language was a mainstay of our family as well. We cussed when we were happy; we cussed when we were sad; we cussed for absolutely no reason at all. Salty language was more like thick brine that neither a night's soak in the kitchen sink nor a back-burner boiling on the stove would temper. Around the home where I lived as a youth, the youngsters were not allowed to use such language without being appropriately reprimanded. But by hearing such language all of the time meant that I knew what all the words meant long before I should have known them. It may sound harsh (and it is not intended to sound so), but the two greatest things that my family gave to me were an ability to laugh and an ability to curse. I have used both of them across the span of my years, I am embarrassed to admit. I was a scrawny little kid and I avoided fights with the big kids because I could cuss better than any sailor. The large kids always assumed that any runt who could cuss like that would likely be able to deliver a good punch so I was never challenged to the school yard fights that most boys have to endure as a rite of passage. I also learned early in life that humor can diffuse a very tense situation. Being funny got me out of countless youthful indiscretions with my peers and out of numerous well-deserved punishments from teachers.

In adulthood, I did much less cussing (in crowds, at least), but I became more and more funny. My friends declare that I have the funniest stories in my repertoire. It is not uncommon to have them pleading with me to tell a story that they've heard time and time again. I can keep the attention of grandkids for hours just finding things to talk and laugh about. Few days pass when I can't get a smile (or a belly busting laugh) out of a co-worker. Some people have concluded that I make things up, but that is not the case. I have an eye for humor and rarely does anything that is funny miss my attention. Many of the people who like me like me because I can usually always find something funny to say.

Many people have suggested that I seriously should think about a career as a comedian although I think that is way, way too much appreciation for my sense of humor. Over the years, I have found humor to be a worthy ally in getting people's attention. Healthy self-deprecation has made a policy foe lower their guard and exposed a weakness in their argument that I noted and later used to win. Being funny can be a medium that makes people comfortable in the presence of a person of position and influence. Humor, rightly and sparsely placed in a sermon, can command interest in and attention to a spiritual truth that I have tried to reveal. Humor has been my best playmate for all of my life.

I also learned to be frugal from my family. My family's preferred pastime was stretching dollars as far as humanly possible. My mother was especially adept at this art. In my preteen and early teen years, I would spend my summers with her where she taught me (by both word and example) to save whatever money I could get my hands on and to always look for bargains, discounts and coupons. To this date, I still cringe at having to pay full price for most things and I rarely buy anything except the essentials for life that is not either on sale, deeply discounted, or thrown in the clearance bin. Though I am prone to spend money very freely on others, I am quite the opposite when it comes to me. I am grateful for having learned those very valuable lessons from my family.

Although my family was as good as any other and much better in some aspects, I never did find my place of comfort in my own family. I still find it very hard to completely understand why. We were fun people. We were happy people. We were people who enjoyed each other. I always felt like I did not fit in. No doubt part of this was the interests that I developed as a kid that were not normative for our family. For example, I was an avid reader in a household where reading, while not discouraged, always took the back seat to a good card game or a popular TV show. While 45's of Motown's finest artists dominated our music preference at home, I rarely missed an episode of the television show, *Hee Haw. Hee Haw* was a country music variety show in my youth. I loved the sometimes funny, sometimes serious stories to be found in the songs sung by country music artists. Though I enjoyed my family, I also found that I liked solitude and being alone too. It would not be uncommon for me to play or read in rooms of the house where no one else was. I did not think it strange to play at the edge of the yard – away from the reach and gaze of my family – rather than find adventures close to the back door. There was a strand of independence in me from my earliest days that I never outgrew. Even today, I enjoy solitude and being alone as much as I enjoy being with good people. Both are a part of my makeup. One of the primary expressions that I remember being drilled into me by my grandmother was to "never let anyone do for you what you can do for yourself." Although I doubt that she meant to include family in that class, but I did. More and more did I learn to depend on myself and less and less on my family.

What is unusual to me about this perspective of my personality is the fact that I spent much of my "by myself time" daydreaming about being in a family. The family of my daydreams was very different from my own. I played with my pretend family in the yard when I was a kid. I was always the father who was married to a beautiful wife and there were varying numbers of children – usually more boys than girls, but when my pretend wife was especially beautiful, I would be the patriarch of a house full of daughters. In my imagination, I was always the best dad ever! I suspect that some of that childish imagination was an attempt to compensate for an absent father. But when I came to the age when I outgrew such childish play, my mind would daydream again about having the perfect family. This imagined family always did the things that my own family did not do and always had all the things that my real family did not have. My mind conceived of exactly what perfection meant in family life and I could re-create it in my head at will.

I started breaking ties with my family after I left for college. It is interesting that my separation from them started in earnest at about the same time that I became serious about having a family of my own. Her name was Grace. I thought she was the sweetest woman in all the world. She was kind, caring, happy, smart and deeply in love with me. We had few things in common from our upbringings: she was from the north and I had been raised in the south. I came from a poor family while she had been raised in a solidly middle class environment. I had always been an excellent student and she didn't see school as the be all and end all of things. Not only were our backgrounds very different, but our personalities were clearly of a ying and yang variety. I was loud while she was always quiet. I liked being the center of attention in a room or at a party while she was the proverbial wallflower. I didn't mind a fight over an issue of injustice or policy while she was prone to forgive and forget and turn the other cheek.

Grace had this beautiful inner quality that radiated outwardly whether she was in an evening dress or an old pair of jeans. What was in her heart and what was in her spirit were never compromised. That inner beauty was the thing that everybody noticed about Grace. But the two things that I most adored about her were these: first, she wanted to have children and, secondly, she would have made the perfect pastor's wife. By that time, I was clear about my ultimate future. I knew that I would end up in the church, probably a pastor. Grace would be the perfect complement to that chosen profession and she had no problem with the idea of being my partner in life and in ministry. With her, my future would be bright and promising. We dated exclusively in college and, though mostly unspoken, each of us knew that, one day after college, we would march down a church aisle having just been pronounced "Reverend and Mrs. Gray." It was only a matter of time before I would get to make my daydreams about family and fatherhood a reality. I could not thank God enough for Grace and I did so every day.

A college athlete friend of mine sustained a rather severe injury to his groin while he was in his senior year. The prospect that his virility was somehow affected worried him tremendously. Nothing is more frightening to a twenty-two-year-old than the suggestion that he is not as virile in practice as he is in his mind. There seems to be something in the psyche of some of the young African-American male by which he mistakenly measures his manhood by his sexual prowess. Doctors had told him that there was a possibility (albeit small) that the injury might affect his ability to have a family one day. It was recommended that certain tests be performed after he had healed to be sure. My jock friend was terrified of knowing if something had happened to make him feel less than the man he knew he was. Over the ensuing weeks, I assured and re-assured him that he was fine, but it seemed that he worried all the more.

In the ultimate act of empathy, I agreed to take the prescribed virility tests that he was scared of taking. I made it into a contest of sorts and I would prove to him that the bookworm (me) had more going on in the manhood department than did the jock (him). I agreed to take the same tests that he had to take in an attempt to build his own confidence and faith. As expected, the results were just as I had been telling him for weeks. He was just fine and the injury and the resulting treatment had done nothing to negatively impact his virility. The surprise was that something unforeseen turned up in my test results. I would be the one who would be unable to father children.

The doctor recited a list of things that could have happened earlier in life to produce these results. I don't recall very much of anything he said. I remember the list being long and the solutions quite minimal. I was told that there were some interventions that could reverse the problems I was having, but the physician wanted to be honest in telling me that he had never seen my particular situation reversed. I lied and told my friend that I had to talk to the doctor about a totally unrelated matter and advised him to go ahead and take the bus for the two-mile trip back to the campus. When the awful consultation with the physician was done, I decided to walk back to school. I stopped at a convenience store and bought the first and only pack of cigarettes I ever bought. I am not sure why I bought them, but I guess I just needed something for company on the walk back to campus.

I was in shock for a few blocks of the long walk home. I was sad for a few blocks. I was devastated for a few blocks. But for most of the walk, I was mad. I was, for the first and only time in my young life, enraged at God. I had been faithful to my call. I had freely given my youth and teen years to His service and not complained at not being able to have a "normal" teenage experience. I had avoided all the typical downfalls of young adulthood to honor my call and be an example to my peers. I had sacrificed much for His Name. If anyone knew how much my heart desired a family and to be father, it was God. I had prayed for that end countless times beginning by including this plea in my "Now I lay me down to sleep" prayers to earnestly and fervently petitioning God in the early days of my ministry. God owed me something for all I had sacrificed and I was mad as hell with Him!

I arrived at the campus having moved through every possible emotion that I contain in my heart and soul, but now I was scared. I could not tell Grace. It would break her heart because I knew how much she, like me, wanted children. How would I face her? How could I ever take away the thing that was so important to her? How could I let her hear the news that would break her heart and ruin our future together? The more I thought about it, the angrier I was with God and at Heaven. I had puffed on more than half the pack and my cursing had at times been quite audible to fellow sidewalk travelers on the walk back to campus. A horrible alliance of fear, stress and humiliation were gaining strength with each step that brought me closer to the campus. By the time I reached the college, my emotions were out of control and the situation had become more than I could bear. I found the converted classroom on campus that pretended to be our chapel. I slipped in, closed and locked the door to the empty and sterile room. I immediately collapsed on the floor. The tears would neither stem nor cease. My anguished prayer/diatribe was not for me nor for Grace nor for healing nor for help. Instead I raised every possible invective against the God I had so loved. Every profane, crude and vile thing that I could think of found its way into that moment of hopelessness and despair. I stopped just short of retreating from my vows to do ministry though I threatened God that I would do so. I declared my own declaration of independence and let God know that He would have my mind and my body. However, He had lost my heart. I could not conceive of how I could honor a God Who could so abuse someone who has been faithful to Him.

I recoil as I remember the deep darkness and despair into which I fell. More than thirty years separate that time from now, but I find myself becoming physically uncomfortable from the mere remembrance. You, dear reader, may never have come to a point of such despair that you have lashed out at God. I sincerely hope that you have not and I sincerely pray that you never will. But I am not the only one whose faith has been shattered and whose hopes have evaporated like the morning dew flees from the rising sun. While I remain embarrassed at my reaction and I regret that my faith was not then as strong as it is now, I am so thankful that my God is strong enough to take my anger and not recoil from me when I was consumed with contempt for His strong will. Like a father takes a screaming toddler into his strong arms and hugs the frustrated child all the more closely the louder the child screams, so did God cradle me in the strength of His love and let me scream and cry and say vile things to Him and about Him. He would not let me go. And He would not let me bear this moment of sorrow and regret alone. It was He and I alone on that chapel floor that dark and gloomy day.

The very One Who had injured me, I reasoned, was also the only One Who could see me through.

It took a long time for me to heal from that body blow to my soul. Things would have been better for me had I sought out someone with whom I could talk. However, the foolish machismo of a nineteen-year-old black male would never let him admit a problem with virility with anyone – not a best friend, not a pastor, not a classmate, not a family member and especially not to a girl whom he loved. I am so sorry that I lacked the maturity and bravery to confront the issue with Grace. Instead of being the man she thought I was, I manufactured some reasons to create clashes between us in the next few weeks. It was all a setup for an intentional breakup. I was mean and I was dishonest and she deserved neither of those. In some warped and immature perspective, I thought it best that I end things where they were. She deserved to love a man who could give her the children that she wanted. And even if I could have afforded further treatment not having Grace in my world made pursuing a medical solution to my problem seem futile.

I mentioned earlier that there was not much communication in my family. We did lot of talking to each other, but very little talking with each other. Our listening was always selective. We heard what we wanted to hear from other family members and we off-handedly dismissed anything that differed from our individual world view. I had come to internalize so many things and talk with no one about my hurts and fears. That was something that I never learned to do while living at home. When I became a minister, my peers found their way to my presence to vent their frustrations, to seek guidance and inspiration and to have a human vault where they could deposit their deepest secrets and be sure that they would never again see the light of day. Unfortunately, I had nowhere that I could deposit my own pain.

My best friend at the time (and ever since sister) was a wonderful woman named Gloria. We met in college and she was the first to befriend me, to look out for me, and to love me so. Glo arranged for my first (and second) work study jobs. She made sure I ate when I was broke and always told me when my newest bargain basement fashion idea was below bargain basement quality. After college, we shared in each other's major life moments: I officiated at her wedding; she had prominent seating at my pastoral installation service. Not many people in the world are as close to me as my big sister Glo, but I suspect that she will be shocked at the reading of this saga. I never really ever told her why Grace and I split. I never told her why she never got to be Aunt Glo. In retrospect, I know in my heart that Glo would have loved me still and perhaps all the more. But I had nothing in my experience to let me know that sharing my hurts would be healing for me.

My biological family was keen at keeping secrets. I was an adult before finding out that my grandmother's first husband (who was my mother's biological father) committed suicide before I was born. Things like this were never discussed. I never knew very much about my father. He was rarely mentioned. Many of the members of my family that I thought were heroic when I was a child turned out to be people with great character and personality flaws: they drank too much, they were unfaithful to their spouses, they beat their wives, and they abused their children. Some of my closest relatives have mental health disabilities. None of these things were ever talked about and much less ever explained. When the veil came off the less than admirable history of my relatives, I think that I felt somehow betrayed. It is not fair to say that I was ever purposely misled. There were just things that we did not talk about. The more I learned about my family heritage, the more I felt that my family members were very much like actors in a play that was my life. I guess we all wear masks, but my issue was that I never really knew what the faces behind the masks were really like. None of us were especially authentic with each other and that especially includes me.

Having abandoned my birth family and not knowing really how to be honest with the family I had created, I was left alone to mourn the loss of the family that I would never produce. I coped by pouring myself into all the other slices in the pie that is life. I graduated early. I poured myself into my first pastorate. I laid the foundation for a purposeful career and profession. I dated several women over the years who would have made loving spouses, but I was careful to keep it all casual. I was always the one who thought it was best to end things. I patched my relationship with God and resigned myself to His will for me. In time, I learned not to focus so much on what I would never have in the future and try to focus exclusively on what I did have in the present.

However, the despair of unrealized hopes never completely evaded me. They hung around like a favored outfit in the back of the closet that does not fit anymore but remains there as a constant reminder of a past that is much too present. For a long while, I would become sad when seeing a young family at the mall or in a restaurant. In my first church, I secretly hated officiating at weddings. I resented standing just inches away from beautiful, happy young people who were about to realize what I never would achieve. I had bandaged my wounds, but they were far from healed.

But God . . .

Amazingly and miraculously God gives us the desires of our hearts. However, they don't always come packaged in the wrapping that we expect nor do they always come in the form that we imagined they would come. The answers to prayer are not always delivered in accord with our personal schedules. Four times over twenty years, four little words resurrected life in the part of my heart that had died.

Randy comes from a very large and loving family who were members of my first pastorate. The Slades are a wonderful clan who love each other and are wholly devoted to each other. The family matriarch is a sweet woman named May. In some ways, May reminds you of Old Mother Hubbard – she had so many children that she did not know what to do. There were always children and/or grandchildren and/or great grandchildren in and around May's house. One reason that I loved to visit was that the environment was always noisy and full of the frolicking of children and the busy-ness of family. It was a safe place for anyone who crossed the threshold and I crossed it often. You could always find something good to eat at May's and somebody had always just done something interesting.

As one of the older boys, Randy helped his mother with keeping things fixed and running around the house. One day, I drove up to find Randy under the hood of a car in the yard. When I blew the horn and his greasy face poked out from under the hood, he had the biggest smile on his face. As always, he was glad to see me. When I came around, there would be something to joke about or something to talk about or maybe a few crumpled dollars would find their way from my pocket to his hands. I got out of the car and was making my way to where he was when my knees nearly buckled. In my spirit, I heard a Voice that was both familiar and strange. It was familiar because I had heard it the night that I gave Christ my life and I remembered it from the night I had been called to preach. It rang in my spirit, not in my ears. I knew this Voice well and I knew the calm and peace that always accompanied that Voice. However, the familiar Voice was strange because there was nothing that I needed to do this time. Previously, when that Voice echoed in my soul, there was something that God wanted from me or something that God wanted me to do. This time there was something that God wanted me to have. The words, *"There is your son, '* echoed in the chambers of my soul. Those words filled my spirit like the train

139

had filled Isaiah's temple. The words were loud as an ocean's waves and as serene as sounds of crickets that fill a summer's night.

Emmanuel (whom we call "Bo") comes from a smaller family. The Williams (mother, two sons and baby girl) came to my first pastorate and into my heart. His mother is an affable and kind woman who works hard and long and faithfully. Whether it was work on the usher's ministry or in the school cafeteria, she worked hard. She instilled that work ethic in all of her children and I saw that and admired that in Bo. His mom was a single mother who did an outstanding job at raising her family. When cash was low, faith was high. She was a fighter and a winner and never gave up. I admired and respected that.

His mother usually took a job with the school system during summer recess. Her regular jobs were cafeteria employee and school bus driver. During the time in question, she was on the custodial staff of one of the schools that was open for summer school. She was busy setting up tables and chairs in a gym on one particular day. I had offered to take Bo along on a two-day beach trip with three other youth in the church. His mother welcomed it and Bo was beside himself anticipating his first trip to the beach. I arrived earlier than expected and found him helping his mom set up tables and chairs. As I waited for them to finish, I could not help but notice that his prescription glasses were broken and had been mended, in several places, with some kind of industrial strength tape. I could not help but wonder if the money I was going to spend on a beach trip would be better spent on a new pair of glasses. The clothes that he would take to the beach were not packed in a suitcase – he didn't own one. Instead an old Vacation Bible School kit box had been adapted as luggage. To me, the beach trip was appearing more and more frivolous with each new discovery.

When his work was done, he started running toward me with all the grace that a young, athletic basketball player has and a large grin that filled his narrow face. As I started to move toward him, my knees temporarily became weak as I was overcome, again, with that Voice. The same four words that I had heard before preceded a profound sense of calm and peace. *This is your son.* We embraced for a moment and I could not help but wonder how he did not recoil from being so close to the fire that had been set aflame in my heart. I quickly realized that my burning bush was mine alone to experience and obey. More than understanding epiphany, Bo just wanted to get to the beach.

Kevin was an adorable, wiry kid who simply adored his pastor. I had baptized each of the Bowe children – two boys and a girl – and they were regular participants in all things "youth" at Shady Grove Baptist Church. Kevin could always be the first one from the pack of kids on the church yard to reach my car when I drove up. He was quick and agile and observant. The first hug of the day would normally be from Kevin. When I visited the house, his brother and sister would migrate to other places in the house while the grown folk talked. Not Kevin. He would be content for long hours sitting on the floor beside me, or in the chair with me, or anywhere close. It seemed that he could never get enough of me and I always looked forward to seeing him.

It was not unusual for me to have lunch at Kevin's school so I knew his friends and his teachers. When other young people would be a little embarrassed that their pastor would be visiting at school, Kevin's teachers often told me that Kevin would be full of energy awaiting my arrival. When Little League started, he expected me in the stands to watch him play. Whenever he came to bat, he would make sure to find me and his mom in the bleachers and grin at us. We acknowledged his glance with the appropriate hoots and hollers that both embarrass and encourage.

During one particular game, his smile was broader than I had seen it before when he came to bat. He looked directly at me. At his glance, it was as if the whole world went silent. I heard nothing of the cheers of proud parents, the instructions being screamed by the coaches, and nothing of the boisterousness that always accompanies Little League. It was as if I went momentarily deaf so as not to miss the still, small Voice that I had heard speak the four words that I had heard thrice before. *"This is your son."*

I do not wish to imply that the father-son relationship with any of my children happened quickly. It did not. It happened gradually with our bonds becoming stronger as time progressed. Over time, without any declaration or ceremony, I became father to these boys. In each case, their biological fathers were not very present in their lives and each of their mothers appreciated my interest in their sons. In time, the community (family, church and school) saw me as their father and, what had initially been thought of as strange, became something natural and wonderful. All of them lived with me at times, but they never were taken from their biological families. Instead their biological families made room for me. The responsibility of helping them get drivers licenses fell to me as did the tongue lashings when they somehow failed to meet curfew. When they returned my car with unexplained dents caused by gnomes who unexpectedly jumped out in front of them, I had both the requisite anger and the requisite patience for a boy that was becoming a man. I stumbled through talks about girls and money and their futures as best I could seeing that I had not had the benefit of receiving those talks from my own father. I loved them deeply and they adored their father.

By the time that I left Shady Grove Baptist Church for my second pastorate at Temple Memorial Baptist Church, my boys had all become men. They were married and were giving me grandchildren with a fierce regularity. One of my proudest moments was getting them all home – without wives and kids – and taking them to High Point to make sure that they were okay with the decision that I had made to move. The ride to and fro was a personal delight as they recounted all the stories from their youth and the things that they had learned from me. It was a very proud and fulfilling moment. I found myself praying in my spirit and apologizing to God for my furor at having thought He had been unkind to me. I knew then, just as I have always known, that God gave me a wonderful family and I am so blessed.

Allen was the unexpected child. He was radically different from his brothers. Randy, Bo and Kevin were members of my church and had grown up in Shady Grove Church. I was the only pastor that they had known. Allen had grown up in Temple Memorial long before I became pastor and was away in college during my early years at Temple. Memorial. The Ingram Family (in which Allen is the middle of all boys) was a stable middle class home with both parents present. My three sons grew up under my tutelage, but Allen was fully grown when the Voice came to me for the fourth time.

Allen's paternal family line was rooted in Temple Memorial Church, but his mother's bloodline was African Methodist Episcopal. Temple Memorial and I were invited to be guests at Turner's Chapel AME Church for Homecoming Worship. I never knew if Allen came home from college that weekend voluntarily or if it was due to the threat of a mother's wrath. In either case, there he was in the number that weekend to be a part of this special event. Whether a volunteer or a draftee, he joined several rows of family members and even more rows of Temple-ites that hot summer afternoon to hear me preach. This was unusual. When Allen was home, Church was not his favorite activity. He often found a reason to get back to school on Sundays or, if he had to endure worship, he would arrive invariably long after the Call to Worship had been offered. Although I knew Allen, I knew his siblings better because they were still living in High Point. I was impressed (and impressed upon) that he was a part of the worship that day that had the unmistakable trappings of a family reunion.

The music by Temple Memorial's choirs was exceptionally good that day and Allen was visibly enjoying the service. This was remarkable because the last pews of Temple Memorial were the best seats in the house for him, but that day he was on the third pew at Turner's Chapel. He was clapping his hands with the congregation and was wholly engaged in the worship. From time to time, he even rose on his feet to encourage the choir in which his mother and aunt were front row singers. I noticed Allen and thought it was wonderfully strange to see his interest and involvement. Just before the sermonic selection was done, I found myself staring at Allen who was literally grinning more broadly than his face. It took me a couple of minutes to reach the pulpit because my legs would not cooperate. Just as Old Testament prophets speak of "the word of the Lord came to me," so did that Voice come to me for the fourth time. *"This is your son."* The familiar calm and peace that always followed the whispers of God in my heart was present as always. I just found it hard to believe since I thought I was done being anyone's father. It was especially troublesome because Allen was an adult and another father was the last thing that I imagined that he needed.

And Allen was my greatest challenge as a father. While his brothers embraced me and reveled in my love for them, it took Allen a very long time to accept my devotion toward him. I guess I wore him down. In time, he would always find time to come by the parsonage when he was home from school. Sometimes the visits were only long enough to collect a sweet potato pie or something Alfredo to take back to school, but they became quite predictable. In time, he (like his brothers) sought my advice and counsel in the weightier issues of life and built his own house of faith on the foundation I helped him lay. He – like Randy, Bo and Kevin – has made my life full and my heart sing.

God does speak in whispers and tones that are specific to our own hearing and healing. But I am also aware that I have followed God's path for my life without having had a dramatic, life changing event.

At times, God has worked in mysterious ways and I have been totally unaware of His activity and my role in His plan. I am convinced that God does not always need our agreement to use us for His purposes. There are times and seasons in life where we are being used and may not even be aware that we are being used.

My very first "son" came to me and I really didn't realize it. I know that sounds strange, but perhaps you will recall something in your life where you saw the Hand of God after the fact. In the moment, you saw nothing out of the ordinary. You just assumed that where you were and what you were doing were merely the result of coincidence or the natural outcome of your simply living your life. Sometimes God is at work just beyond the veil. He is far enough away not to gain our notice, but close enough to place us in the right place at the right time to be an instrument of His love or His grace. Thus, meet Foxx.

One of my best friends from college, Cherie, had a calling to work with youth. I am not sure that either she nor I understood that as recent twenty-something college graduates. We may have been too preoccupied with our futures and our fortunes to even realize that God was working in us and through us. We simply knew that there were things that made us happy and things that we liked to do with and for people. That was motivation enough.

Cherie had (and still has) the largest heart of perhaps anyone that I have ever known. Sharing came so naturally to her and taking on others' burdens was second nature. Fresh out of college, she started a gospel choir of youth in the community. In the process, she collected a motley crew of teenagers upon whom she could lavish her love and attention. She actually created a safe place and sanctuary for these youth who needed a little extra attention and guidance. Her house was always full of kids. At Cherie's house, these young folk were in a constant state of singing, or eating, or fussing. Sometimes all at the same time.

I often found myself at Cherie's house to help and just be near in case somebody needed something. Believe me when I say that someone always needed something – a ride, a few dollars, a meal, a pair of shoes, something. Exactly how she and I provided so much for so many as two broke, recently graduated college students, I will never know. Except for the grace of God, there can be no other explanation. In addition to being a helper for Cherie, I was also something of a role model for the young men in her group. There were things that they would tell me that they would never tell her. I could also perceive certain things about the young men in Cherie's care that Cherie missed. Being around was not burdensome at all; it was a great joy.

Foxx was an adorable teenager whose bright smile and gushing joy made him exceptional in a lot of ways. He was a part of the inner circle of Cherie's choir and it was not uncommon for him to be around more than most. On those nights where we got back from a singing engagement too late for me to make it home, Foxx would have the couch and I would take the floor in the living room. Somebody else's breathing would be heard from an arm chair and bodies lay strewn all around the house. During one of those sleepovers, Foxx and I talked about his life and struggles. For a young man, he was carrying weights much too heavy for his age and experiences much too adult for a child. At some point during the night amid our whispering back and forth, he told me "I wish you were my Daddy."

I didn't think very much of it then. I don't recall even responding. I guess that my impression was that he either did not mean it or he did not have a clue how unprepared I was to take on the responsibility that a father would have to assume. Unlike the Voice that I would hear at other times in my life, I felt nothing spiritual nor powerful about that moment. It could have been that I was so immature in my own spiritual formation that I could not see the forest for the trees. It very likely could have been that I was not as committed to living a life of service to others then as I am now. Or it simply could have been the fact that God didn't really need my assent or my knowledge to use me for purposes larger than my own life.

But over time and little by little, I assumed the role of being a father to him. It started with my seeing that he got back and forth to school and to his job at a biscuit joint. It moved to helping him buy his first car. It progressed to the inevitable high school things of games, and proms, and grades. Foxx would tell people that I was his dad and I accepted the role little by little. In reality, it never did fully dawn on me until he left for college in West Virginia. With him away at college, I realized that a great emptiness and deep void had come into my life. The evidence was a large hole in my heart and a grayness that entered into my world.

That's not the only time that sons have come to my family crest without the Godly pre-authorization to which I had become accustomed. It happened with Thomas who, in a text message one day, asked if I would mind if he no longer called me "Doc," but started calling me "Dad." It happened again with Jeremy who, when I least expected it, would meet me for lunch or supper at the parsonage and ask, "How's my old man doing?" With Joe, it occurred during an awful time of my criticizing a sermon manuscript that he had bought to me when he said, "You are sure hard on your son." With LaMont, it resulted from his back and forth debate about what his young children should call me: grandpa or grandfather. With Terrell, it occurred after taking him to a doctor's appointment and spending the day with him to allay his nerves about his diagnosis. A few weeks later, his text messages started with the word "Pops." In each of these circumstances (and others), I was totally unaware of the ministry I was doing nor of the effect I was having on the young people around me. I was just "doing what I do" and being who I am. For far too long, I thought that ministry was only what I did in the pulpit or in my role as a pastor. How wrong I was! However, it may be that it is in those times of our being totally unaware that we may be more of an instrument of God's use than we are in any other context.

I really believe that we spend far too much time and brainpower trying to figure out what it is that God wants us to do. I spent a significant part of my early ministry trying to figure out that same thing. My prayers were more often about begging God for some clear sign of what I was supposed to be doing. I wondered if I was on the right path. I was afraid that I was moving away from God's will as opposed as toward it. As I grew in faith and practice, I became convinced that if one concentrates on what God is calling us to be, we will stumble into what God wants us to do. If you can figure out that God is calling you to be kind, or passionate, or organized, or reflective, it will not take long to find out what it is that God wants you to do. Actually, those things will come to you. Whether we arrive at the revelation of what we are to do because we have literally heard the whisper of God in our heart or if we come to that place by tripping and stumbling over our own shortcomings and unawareness, what is important is that we come to discover what it is that God really wants us to do.

I struggle still with exactly why I abandoned the family that loved and nurtured me. I suspect that I will never really know. But I do know that the larger family that God has allowed me to piece together has really been the work of God. I am comfortable in the shoes that God has given me to walk in and I am in no ways tired. God has somehow, in God's own miraculous way, given me much in family, in fatherhood and in love than I could ever have imagined. Thanks be to God.

"Lessons for Ministry"

1. God's claim on your life is both for your public and private ministry. God wants to use you for a meaningful and enduring

purpose as a pastor, a minister, a chaplain, a church worker, but He also wishes you to be a minister in quiet, unassuming, and non-public ways. In some instances, you might never be known for the ministry of the heart as you extend the love of Christ to others, but in many ways this is the most fulfilling part of being called to ministry.

2. Great purpose can come out of great pain. Though all of us seek to avoid periods of pain and suffering, it may take pain and loss to position you for some higher purpose in life and in ministry. Before crops can be planted, the ground must be broken. Tilling is a hard and violent process that turns the soil and breaks the ground. Without this breaking and disturbance, seeds that are to be planted will not germinate; they will not grow; they will not produce fruit. Entertain the possibility that your pain has a purpose even (and especially if) the purpose hides from you in the present.

3. Try to believe that the people who love and trust you will love and trust you even when you feel broken and helpless. Do not try to carry the bitter burden of the cross alone. While not everyone is worthy of the knowledge of your private struggles, be sure to cultivate a relationship with a few people who will not exploit your weaknesses, but will support you in your weak times.

4. God is God enough to give us what we desire, but – because He is God – He knows how to best give us what we desire even if it comes in unexpected packages.

CHAPTER 11

"... FROM PELHAM ..."

THE ONLY CHURCH that I ever really thought should have called me as pastor was a church I did not serve. The Trinity Baptist Church of Danville, Virginia was the best church in the world, I thought. They were without a pastor and somehow I had been invited to preach while they searched for a pastor. After my first Sunday, I had convinced myself that I was the pastor for them and they were the church for me. It is interesting how easily we transfer our own wants and desires into a self-convinced truth that whatever we want has to be God's will and perfect plan. Apparently, I was convinced, but the members of Trinity Church were not. After weeks of preaching and posturing, the Church called another minister as their pastor. I was devastated that they did not even show me the courtesy of granting me an interview. I was sincerely crushed by the experience. In retrospect, I completely understand why Trinity did not call me. I was only twenty years old and I was still in college. I had no seminary training and my soon-to-be-had college degree would not be in religion and philosophy, but in social work and English. While I had developed a fairly good reputation as a young preacher, I knew very little about being a pastor. Fortunately, Rev. Arthur R. White had given me many points and pointers, but I really was not ready for the challenge of being a pastor at a well-established church like Trinity.

I had won the support of Deacon Lindsey Fountain, Trinity's senior deacon. Deacon Fountain had taken a liking to me. It was his sheer force of will that kept me coming to Trinity. I would later discover that the other deacons wanted the Church to use the Sunday morning preaching hour to hear candidates who were better suited for the pastorate and who had a reasonable chance of being called. However, Deacon Fountain insisted on bringing me back multiple Sundays in a month. I never knew exactly why Deacon Fountain was pushing my candidacy so. Perhaps it was because he truly liked me and saw some potential in me. Maybe it was a repeat of the Bryant's experience in which Deacon Fountain's influence in the church could be maintained by the call of a young, inexperienced pastor. Whatever his motivations, he was genuinely concerned about how devastated I was over having been rejected.

A note was taped to the door of my dorm room at 21 Bishop Hall. A dorm mate had scrawled a message for me to call L. Fountain. It was a Friday and I returned the call. Deacon Fountain simply told me that there was someone that he wanted me to meet. He would pick me up on Saturday morning. We met at the appointed place and time and we drove to the Almagro community. Almagro was another primarily African-American neighborhood in Danville. If Holbrook Street was where the prominent blacks had once lived, Almagro was where the masses of working class people lived. At the center of Almagro was the barber shop owned by John Thomas Bethel. Like Fountain, Bethel was the senior deacon of his church. The two deacons were the best of friends and, unbeknownst to me, I was about to have the strangest job interview I ever had in my life. Apparently Fountain had told Bethel about me and about the unfortunate fact that Trinity chose to call another pastor instead of me. Fountain wanted Bethel to arrange a preaching opportunity for me at Bethel's church, Shady Grove Baptist Church.

I walked into the barber shop with Deacon Fountain that morning and was warmly greeted by Deacon Bethel. Bethel took one of the two barber chairs in the shop and Fountain took the other. I was left to stand near the soda machine that never dispensed sodas. It served as a kind of gigantic night light in the darkness of an Almagro night. And the two old friends went at it. The conversation went along these lines:

Fountain: "Bethel, this is the young preacher I was telling you about. The folk at Trinity voted in somebody else and I think you all should give him a try."

Bethel: "Well, if y'all don't want him, why should we want him?"

Fountain: "Bethel, I done told you he is a good young preacher. He will make you proud out at your church. Plus, he is in school over at Averett College so you don't have to pay him much."

Bethel: "Saving money is always good, Fountain. But he looks too young for us."

Fountain: "You was young a thousand years ago, Bethel, but you outgrew that and he will too."

Bethel: "Okay, Fountain. I will see what I can do. You want a haircut now?"

Fountain: "No. I'll come back later after I take him back to school."

With that, my first interview for a pastoral position was done. Deacon Fountain rose from the barber's chair in which he had sat, gestured for me to follow him, and we left. No question was asked to me by Deacon Bethel: he did not ask my name, where I was from, or what I was studying in college. I was witness to a debate between two friends who seemed unaware that the subject of their argument was standing in the room. When I got back to the campus, Deacon Fountain assured me that I would hear from Deacon Bethel very soon. I got out of Deacon Fountain's car in the high humidity of a southern Virginia August. In the middle of October when the heat and humidity of August had given way to the cool breezes of fall, there was another note taped to my dorm room. This time a dorm mate had scrawled a message to call J. T. Bethel at a number that he had given. Had the "interview" not been strange, I doubt I would even have remembered who J. T. Bethel was. I had a suspicion that Bethel was someone I would never forget.

There had apparently been several discussions about me (outside my presence this time) between the two deacon friends. Deacon Bethel had either been converted or he had surrendered his will to Fountain's. Whatever the cause, I had been invited to give a sermon at Shady Grove Baptist Church across the line in North Carolina on the first Sunday of November, November 2, 1980. Bethel had apparently learned a lot about me because he knew I owned no car and he agreed to pick me up on the Sunday in question at the same place and time that Fountain had done so many times prior.

After not being called to Trinity, I convinced myself that I would never again open my heart to the call of a church. It had cost too much of my reserve of pride and was far too emotional for me to endure that again. I had decided, by the time that my invitation to preach at Shady Grove came around, that I would hedge my bets in life. I was going to attempt to win admittance to the School of Social Work at Virginia Commonwealth University in Richmond, Virginia. A Master's degree in Social Work would insure that I would have consistent employment. I had decided that I was going to simultaneously pursue a Master of Divinity degree at Virginia Union University School of Theology. This is the seminary where my then-pastor Arthur R. White had graduated. The M. Div. degree, I reasoned, would come in handy if a church (unlike Trinity) ever recognized my "true worth." I knew that this was truly an ambitious plan. However, considering that I was a semester and a half from completing my four-year degree in three years, there were the signs that I could do the impossible. I would graduate with over 130 semester hours when only 120 were required for a degree. As well, I would have a double major in two entirely different disciplines. These things made me think that pursuing two graduate degrees in two separate graduate schools was entirely plausible. I had done all of the above while being active in my church and holding down two work study jobs (one in the theatre arts department and one in the registrar's office), tutoring Vietnamese refugees in English, regularly preaching in a prison ministry and preaching at any church that would invite me as a guest speaker. VCU and VUU would seem almost like a holiday vacation compared to the pace and schedule I was keeping in undergraduate school. I was completely consumed by what I could do at the next stage of my life; I had not considered what God wanted me to be.

In retrospect, I look back over those fast paced days during my last year of college and realize that I was far too focused on what God wanted me to do and not focused enough on what God wanted me to be. Did God want me to do ministry in the context of being a social worker? Did God want me in a more traditional form of ministry as in the pastorate? Did God want me to teach English and have a ministry to youth? Did God want me to build on my prison ministry experience and try the chaplaincy? I was consumed with what I was to do, but my college years were shaping me into what God wanted me to be. I had learned more than social work and English at Averett. I had learned the grace of giving, the joy of helping others, and the power of encouraging others. I know now that I was being called to be a giver, a helper, and an encourager. I had to learn how to be patient with people, to be accepting of people who were different, and to love people. God was calling me to be the kind of person who wore those attributes easily like a well fitted suit. These were the things that I was called to be and, as a consequence of my becoming comfortable in what I was called to be, I came to understand what I was to do. Had I understood then as I do now, I would have known that what I was to do was to be in a calling where I could help people in a context where I could love them, encourage them, build them, and glorify God.

So the first Sunday in November came without very much fanfare. I honestly did not see that this North Carolina congregation would do any differently than the Virginia congregation had done. I resolved to not allow myself to become attached to or emotionally involved with the good people at Shady Grove. I just saw it as a preaching opportunity, nothing more. God intended something more, much more.

Apparently, Deacon Bethel had learned from Deacon Fountain's mistake. Instead of having other more serious candidates to preach at Shady Grove as Fountain had allowed at Trinity, I was pretty much the only preacher that Shady Grove heard from the first Sunday in November until the third Sunday in February. Deacon Bethel was determined not to allow the Church to have very much of a choice. In his mind, the only acceptable choice would be me or me. This did not sit well with the congregation, but Bethel was relentless. In February 1981, Shady Grove Baptist Church extended a call to me to become their next pastor and I accepted.

I found out later that it had not been an easy call. Deacon Bethel had used all of the Church political capital that he had amassed over many years of being a member and then deacon and finally the chair of deacons in that church. The church was clearly divided over the issue of calling me. The dissension had been so strong that Deacon Bethel had to surrender the role of presider at the Church meeting where I was voted in to our Association's moderator, Dr. E. L. Kirby. Though Dr. Kirby had been in many boiling hot Church fights over the years, he later told me that my call had been one of the worse. After several ballots and parliamentary maneuvers, a compromise was reached: a slim majority of people voted to extend a call to me, but I would have a non-renewable twelve-month contract. It was literally the best that could come out of that situation. It was a totally acceptable arrangement to me. I needed a break from school and the frenetic life I was leading. I would pastor the church for a year, save some money, buy maybe two or three suits and maybe make a down payment on a car. When the year was done, I would be off to Richmond to pursue dual Master's degrees. Seeing that I was graduating in three years anyway, the year at Shady Grove would not put me behind in my life plan. However, what was intended to be a one-year contract turned into a seventeen-year love affair. I fell madly in love with Shady Grove and they, in turn and in time, fell in love with me. Having now been away from that Church for almost as many years as I stayed, I still believe that my time at Shady Grove was my most productive and happiest time in my ministry. I really do thank God every time I remember them.

It did not take me very long to figure out that I had a real mess on my hands. The Church was in shambles – spiritually, financially and its local reputation had plummeted. Church fights were commonplace in business meetings and on the church parking lot. The fighting was verbal on the inside of the building and sadly occasionally physical on the outside of the building. The Church was dominated by two principal families – one family lived primarily in Virginia and the other family primarily lived in North Carolina. The affiliation to blood (as it relates to family ties) and dirt (as it relates to geography) were the principal factors determining which side of almost every debate that members fell. Of course, there were exceptions to the rule because both families' roots were in North Carolina. Families are notorious for disagreeing with each other. The unifying force of family is often tenuous and does fail. Sometime the fighting was just for fighting's sake – it didn't always matter what family you were from or in which state you paid taxes. In general, the North Carolina-Virginia state line was also the dividing line for my congregation.

My predecessor had left the Church under very unfortunate circumstances. His ouster had caused an even deeper divide in the Church. The "Virginia" family had been the catalysts leading to the dismissal of the previous pastor. The "North Carolina" family had supported the former pastor and was incensed that they had been outmaneuvered in the meeting that codified his resignation. I never really knew what the problems were that led to the fateful decision. There was no moral issue or financial issue involved. It may very well have been that the good pastor merely became a pawn on the chess board created by these opposing forces. If things had been bad before, they were considerably worse by the time that I arrived. Adding to the dissent was the fact that the "Virginia" family had been the primary supporters of my being called to the Church. This only infuriated the "North Carolina" family and made them automatically suspicious of the new pastor. The divide was so great (and so literal) that the families actually sat on opposite sides of the chancel. If, during my sermon, I looked to the right, I would look into the disappointed faces of the "North Carolina" family. If looked to the left, I would look into the gloating faces of the "Virginia" family. I spent my first few weeks preaching while staring at the clock on the center back wall of the sanctuary. It literally took only a few Sundays to discover just how deep and strong the divide was. Not only was the worship service a time to "show your colors," it was a time to align with whatever side had claimed your devotion.

I was blessed to have figured out that the dissention in the Church had nothing to do with me personally. My call was simply the precipitating factor that made the raw emotions rise to the surface in the congregation. Had I internalized the discord as being personally directed at me, I doubt that I would have survived the first year. Church fights and disputes are rarely actually about what the fights and disputes claim to be about. They tend to have very deep roots that go back in time and into the dark ground of secrets that nourish the dissent. These battles can simmer for a long time just below the surface and some external factor (like the call of one pastor and the dismissal of another) can be the trigger that sets off an explosion. A minister would do well to learn the history of a church to which one is called to serve. The history of the church is more than what is published and read on the obligatory Church anniversary services. The real history is the often unwritten, but is often a whispered about past of a church that influences its present.

I knew that I had to quickly find some common ground among the competing interests. And I had to find it fast. There was the real possibility that disagreements might turn into the physical fights that had happened prior to my being called. I did not want things to degrade to such a state. I soon figured out that everyone was worried about the Church's debt. The Church had been remodeled before I was called and the departed pastor left a debt of over $40,000.00. For a struggling rural congregation, a forty-thousand-dollar mortgage was as daunting a challenge as forty million. Getting rid of the debt was something that everyone could agree on. I made that a point of emphasis and began to develop ideas about how we could do away with the mortgage. I have learned that one of the first registers of discontent among Church people is that they find ways to withhold their financial support from the ministry. This was already beginning to happen and I saw a crisis looming in the distance. The call to retire the mortgage had a unifying effect on the warring families (albeit true that they were at odds on just about everything else) and it gave a reason for dissatisfied members to release the funds that they had been withholding.

The second unifying theme that I developed was giving attention, love and energy to the children and youth of the Church. Seeing that I was only twenty years old when Shady Grove called me, I was young enough to relate and enjoy the young people. Children sense when adults truly care for them and about them. Once they realize this, they love those adults passionately. I placed all my chips on the idea that it would be hard for the adults to hate someone that their children adored. As I began to include the youth in worship services, started a Sunbeam Choir of the cutest and tiniest voices, became a regular lunch buddy at school, and instituted various events and ministries geared toward the young, things began to change. Just as I had thought, I was finding more and more acceptance by the feuding adults through the attention and devotion I was showing for the children and that the children were showing for me.

This was no plot or plan. For me, it was genuine. It was a natural extension of who I was at the time. I was young and it was easy for me to relate to the young. I knew what they liked and what they did not. I knew their music, their dress and their TV shows. I was becoming their "go to" adult with whom they would trust things that they would never tell their parents. To them I was cool and they were cool to me. The adults in the congregation could not miss the obvious connection and love. I made their children happy and that made them happy. Happy begets happy.

The other prong of my approach involved the eldest members of our parish. Having been raised by my grandmother and having been in a context where older people were a staple, I was at ease around older and old people. I enjoyed hearing their stories and I reveled in their strong faith. I visited the elderly often and made it known that I had been with the sages of the Church. I picked up on some of their phrases and added them to my own vocabulary. I tried to remember birthdays and other special occasions. The more I loved them, the more they loved me. In time, they refused to remain silent among the attacks that came my way because one side or the other disagreed with something I had done or proposed or instituted. A tribal nature still exists in the

African-American church which makes even the fiercest of opponents respect the opinion of the elders. More and more, the elders were liking the young boy who was their pastor.

The elders of the church were turning out to be a bottomless reservoir of information about the unspoken history of the church. From that reservoir, I drank often and deeply. As I earned their trust, they told me the "secret" things that no one discussed. I came to understand how prior relationships among members colored their current feelings. I was told who hated who, who loved who, who didn't care about who and who was who. I never told the things that the elders shared with me in confidence, but this knowledge was immensely helpful in understanding why so many things were as they were. It was that knowledge which was so essential in helping me know what things might work well and which ones might not.

While these things were playing out, I was giving great attention to my preaching. I abandoned most of my Old Testament sermons. The stories of conquering this people or that people inevitably led both sides to incorrectly assume that the sermon was a prophecy of one side of the sanctuary conquering the other side. A text about the wrath of God would be misinterpreted as the fate of whomever was mad with whomever. David slaying Goliath was a vindication of each side claiming to be David while declaring the other side has to be Goliath. For my early preaching, I focused on the New Testament with its themes of love, compassion, forgiveness, justice and devotion to God, not to people. There is a certain forward look to the New Testament that became prominent in my preaching. My subtext was that our torrid past was not as important as our promising future as a Church. This preaching plan began to pay off, bit by bit, sermon by sermon, person by person.

The word began to spread about this "boy preacher" who did so much to care for his members, who loved children, who revered the aged and who preached well and laughed heartily. In time, visitors began to show up and, in time, visitors became members. The growth of the church was another unifying factor. The warring factions shared their pride at being a part of a growing church even if one side held nearly half of the congregation in contempt. New members meant that the traditional balance of power was destined to change. I did not have to force any shift; time would do that.

Then the funerals started. I have listened to some pastors speak of "timely" deaths in their congregations that seem to have solved church problems by removing the driving influence of a certain mindset or opposition. I never really felt that way because my experience is that the opposers keep coming. I saw funerals as very special opportunities to show pastoral care and for the congregation to show love. All swords were put down when a funeral happened. Folk who did not like each other could work together on the kitchen committee to make sure a grieving family had a nice "repast" after a funeral. People who normally competed against each other could work together on the cemetery committee or as floral bearers for a funeral. Folk who genuinely disliked each other could empathize with each other when grief came to visit.

I took to the business of pastoral care to bereaved families with a passion. I was almost obsessed by being "present" with bereaved families. If a member was critically ill in the local hospital, I would rush to the bedside. If I heard that a member passed, I would make it to the house as soon as humanly possible. Over the course of my first two or three years at the church, I cultivated the habit of meeting families at the funeral home to assist in arranging the final services for their loved ones. I made sure that the families' first viewing – the private viewing of a deceased person by the immediate family before the corpse is publicly viewed – was scheduled at a time that I could be present. I would stay as long as they stayed: ten minutes or two hours. I visited the home where the family gathered daily between the time of the death and the funeral service. I made sure to make a few calls in the days immediately following the burial as well. I befriended the owners of a local funeral home and became their "unofficial" chaplain which meant I would be the "minister on call" for those instances where an unchurched person had a chapel service. I began to hang out at the funeral home and help out when I could. My growing and deepening friendship with that funeral home led to my being able to extract some concessions on the price for services and products when members of our church used that particular funeral home. As well, I volunteered to help out at a local florist when demand was high and, in lieu of compensation, I could always get some extra creative touch for our members' floral arrangements when loved ones died.

What I was learning from this perhaps "over the top" attention to grieving families was that the presence of the minister really matters. In the years before I turned 25, I have to admit that I did not always have the ability to turn out a good phrase for every occasion that I was called upon to be a pastor. I learned that there are times that merely being present says the right thing. The power of being present is something that I learned in the earliest days of my pastoral ministry and it was a habit that I was never able to break.

Though it took some years to fully realize, I wanted funerals to be dignified, reflective and spiritual experiences. I was not very patient with families who wanted to stage large, near theatrical presentations that did little to honor the life of the dearly departed. I became a stickler for things like starting on time, having things in place and conducting the service with an eye toward exceptionalism. While these things may seem obvious to the reader as things that ought to happen, they were not the standard for the small, rural community in which I served as my first parish.

I went to great pain to write funeral eulogies that were personal and powerful. I understood that there would be some members of families who were not churchgoers attending the funerals where I preached. It was important to make a good impression and sow the seed that might encourage that person to try Church again or for the first time. I made sure that every eulogy was different and I took to preaching from the non-traditional texts. I sought to find some parallel, some point of comparison about the deceased and the Bible passage that I had chosen. It was important to be honest. When the deceased's relationship with God was questionable, I did not try to "preach them into heaven." I sought to celebrate the humanity that God had created and the divinity that made the person unique. When the deceased was obviously a pillar of the faith, I did not attempt to canonize them in my eulogies, but I tried to present their humanity and their struggles, their quirks and uniqueness. I may have done my best preaching at funerals in my first years at Shady Grove.

My early emphases of nurturing young people, revering our elders, unifying the church on a mortgage elimination and making funerals unique were paying off with grand results. Noticing the growing positive feeling for the new pastor in the church and in the community, Deacon Bethel used his influence to persuade the church to purchase the first automobile that I ever owned. For my birthday in the spring of my first year, the Shady Grove Baptist Church gave me the keys to a Chevrolet Monte Carlo. It was fully paid and they told me to use it until I could do better. I loved that car passionately and I loved the idea that it was a symbol of the love that the people I served had for me. I used the car to expand my pastoral ministry. With it, there were no limits to how "present" I could be for our members.

Although the early days of my pastorate were very full with pastoral things, my life at school was also quite demanding. I was still a senior in college and I was fulfilling the demands of a required internship in medical social work at the local hospital. I tried to keep up with the campus social life as best that I could. I surrendered one of my college work-study jobs to supplement the yet limited compensation I was receiving at Shady Grove. It was in these days that I developed my unfortunate and unhealthy habits as a workaholic. Days off were virtually impossible because when I was off from church, I was on at school. When I had a lull in school work, I needed extra work study hours. When the work study assignment trailed off, I found more things to do at Church. For my entire ministry, I have an established pattern of working far past the normal forty-hour work week. Long nights and all-nighters have never been rare for me. I regret that I never learned the value of rest and retreat in my early ministry. Now the result of doing too much all of the time is apparent in the health issues that I face. While I am strongly convinced that the course I took in my first pastorate was the right course to take, I wish I had understood that I did not have to follow that course at breakneck speed. That is a pattern and way of life that I have never been able to break.

My first year at Shady Grove was a grand success. I graduated in May, only three months after I had been called. My internship as a medical social worker in the spring turned into a full-time job in the summer. The church was showing signs of growth and our influence in the community was growing. I was learning a lot in the pastorate, but I kept in the back of my mind the fact that I would be moving on come February. The monthly church business meeting of February 1982 brought about a unanimous vote to extend my twelve-month contract for another year. The annual ritual of "voting on the pastor" continued for eight years. The votes were always unanimous and on the eight-year vote, after a unanimous vote in the affirmative, somebody made a motion that the annual vote be discontinued and that I would serve indefinitely as the pastor of the Shady Grove Baptist Church. Again the vote was unanimous and this vote was met with cheers and heartfelt emotion. With each annual vote, I would tell myself that graduate school was just one more year away. By the time that the annual vote was suspended, I knew in my heart that I had found my place in ministry and in life. I knew that graduate school and moving on to another church and city were too far distant for me to imagine or contemplate.

I had spent the first few years at Shady Grove intently focused on the church and its growth and development. However, by year eight and the suspension of the annual vote, I was well on the way to making the influence of our church felt throughout the community. I was a strong supporter of our local Association and, in the early 1990's, I sought and won a position as one of the Vice Presidents of our state convention. Community meetings were a staple on my calendar and I was very intentional about forming friendship with other pastors and establishing alliances with other churches. In the late 1980's, I was one of the few full-time resident pastors in our entire county. I was the only fulltime African-American pastor in our corner of the Caswell County, North Carolina woods.

Civic engagement and community organization came as natural extensions of my pastoral ministry. As I knew our members and their needs more intimately, I became interested and involved in the things that would make their lives better. Politics can be and is a dirty business, but I had to become involved because it was the mechanism by which services and opportunities could be opened to the members of our church and to the communities in which our members lived. I earned quite a reputation as a whistleblower and was not timid in exposing inequalities among communities in the county and injustices turned upon people of color. I did research on candidates for public office and peppered them with questions about the matters facing the African-American community. In time, my endorsement (or lack thereof) became a measurable factor in determining what local politicians won election to office. When I believed that a particular candidate would support the issues that would enhance the quality of life for people, I supported their election with every fiber of my being. After their election, those same fibers kept their campaign promises before them. Failing to advance the promises upon which they were elected might well mean that I would work for their defeat the next time around. Although I had moved from Danville to Caswell County to live, I was sensitive to the political issues on both sides of the state line. Although I could not vote for Virginia politicians because I lived in North Carolina, I held their feet to the fire to keep the campaign promises that they made to our members who lived in Virginia.

My ministry to youth had made me a frequent visitor to the local schools. Most principals knew me and I was always being invited to this program or that event at school. More and more, the invitations to school-based events were being extended when young people in our church were not directly involved. In some ways, I was becoming the youth pastor for the community. It was a natural outgrowth of my ministry to our church's youth. I'd have lunch with a student in our church and meet their friends who were in other churches. It became normal to inquire how their friends were doing. Frequently, kids who were best friends at school persuaded their parents to come to our church. Another phenom was occurring. The more present I was in the schools, the more I became a resource person for children and families in crisis. I might visit the school to see about one of my kids and have an administrator to ask me to intervene with another family whose children were having problems in school or with the school. In time, I became an ombudsman for school personnel who felt that the school system was treating them unfairly. The schoolhouse was as comfortable a field of service for me as was the church house.

In the early 1990's, I took the political plunge and ran for a seat on the local board of education. I had thought about it for some time and there were community voices who felt that the status quo did not represent nor support the needs of children who were struggling in school. The racial issues were prevalent and children of lower income families were not being well served by the system. I decided to challenge the long time school board chairman for his district seat. It was a bold move since this individual had never been challenged before and it was doubly traumatic for the county that an African-American might unseat the chairman. I made a heroic effort, but lost in a narrow election. In many ways, the loss was a win. My influence was substantially heightened and my opinions on public school issues were sought after. By the time that an at-large seat came open two years later, I was well positioned to mount a countywide challenge. I did and I won easily.

I approached my role as a school board member with the same tenacity that I had approached my coming to Shady Grove as pastor ten years earlier. I threw myself into the work and always out-visited, out-studied, out-learned and out-maneuvered my colleagues on the board. I always did research on upcoming topics so I could intelligently discuss (and often debate) the merits of proposals coming before the board. I got to know school personnel personally and invited their opinions about issues coming before the board. I knew what parents wanted and was able to express what was on their hearts to colleagues who were generally uninterested in what parents of African-American children wanted.

It did not take long for the majority on the board to band together to press policies into place. I was infamous for being the only member to vote "no" on an important issue. Those stances were seen as an affront to the unity of the board; I saw those "no" votes as representing my constituency. In time, my colleagues took delight in being able to easily override my objections to an issue. They knew that if they could endure the questions I would pepper them or the presenters with, they would ultimately be able to put their policies in place with a 6-1 vote. What they did not know is that the public votes during school board meetings was not really where I was effecting change. Change was happening because of my growing public posture and influence. Ideas could be instituted or de-railed long before they reached the school board policy-making level. By showing up and offering my thoughts to the right school personnel, things were made better for children and employees. The mere threat of a "hell raising" at a board meeting or in a school setting was more than enough to influence the outcome of a decision that adversely affected children. My colleagues thought that they were publicly humiliating me by out voting me on a policy matter when, in actuality, the matters that really made a difference to me had been handled long before a school board issue.

I had been asked on several occasions to run for higher office, but that never interested me. My ministry to young people in the area was an important part of my ministry. I could not see making a difference for them on the county's board of commissioners or as a state representative. I was being what God wanted me to be and the result of knowing what I was to be was that I also knew what I was to do.

I am not exactly sure how I developed the list, but after my first successful year at Shady Grove I came up with a list of top churches and pastors in North Carolina. I had a simple plan in place. I wanted to meet each of these pastors and visit them at the churches. My idea was to find out what they were doing well in their churches and then attempt to replicate that in my own. My pattern did not vary. I would call the pastor's office, make an appointment, show up on the appointed day and time, introduce myself and attempt to find out everything the pastor might be willing to share. I found them to be very open and willing to help a young pastor. They were very open with their stories about their journeys in ministry. They were glad to talk about their stellar programs and growing ministries. I was impressed as any young minister would be. I was impressed to have won a few hours of their time and impressed that they would tell me so much of their life and ministry stories.

It did not take very long for me to understand an important fact. Each of these ministers had developed programs, ministries and services that grew out of a need in the congregation and community. If members had sub-standard housing, the church became involved in building affordable housing. If the public school lacked for low income children, daycare centers would be opened to give children in the community the extra help they needed to be ready for school. If seniors had nowhere to go while their caregiving children were away at work, a church started an elder care program. I had started out with the intention of finding successful ministries across the state and come back to Pelham and implement what I had seen. What I learned was that I needed to build our ministry at Pelham based on what was unique about Pelham and its people. That was an invaluable lesson and it has guided me throughout my ministry.

This top list of churches and ministries had another good effect. I developed some friendships with some very prominent and powerful African-American preachers as a result of my working my way down the list. These friends opened many doors across the state for ministry for me. I could depend on their advice and counsel when I needed it. They frequently told me about a good book to read, a good conference to attend, and a good sermon thought to develop. And they were always telling me about vacant pulpits and encouraging me to think about life after Pelham. For the most part, I appreciated the fact that they had higher aspirations for me than I had for myself, but I was happy and fulfilled in Pelham. I wasn't interested in serving elsewhere.

In 1988, Dr. L. L. Macon died. Dr. Macon was the legendary pastor of the Temple Memorial Baptist Church in High Point. He was known as an extraordinary preacher and he had conducted a revival for me at Shady Grove in Pelham. When the requisite mourning period was over and applications for the pulpit were requested, I applied. I did it more out of a sense of wanting to get a feel for what the rest of the church world was like. I was being strongly urged by pastors across the state to do so. I applied, interviewed and preached at Temple Memorial and I was impressed. The church building was significantly larger than my own. There was a tremendously larger congregation. The worship and the music were delightful. The people were very warm during my visits. But I knew that being in my early 30's coupled with not having a seminary degree were real barriers to receiving such a call. I was not surprised when, given two names for their next pastor, the good people of Temple Memorial did not choose me. I quickly put the sugar plum dreams I had had of being an urban pastor out of my mind and resumed (with a vengeance) my ministry at Shady Grove.

A strange sense began to come to me a few years after I had applied to become Temple Memorial's pastor. It was a combination of feelings – a feeling that I wasn't really doing my best work at Shady Grove, a feeling that I had become too comfortable in ministry, and a feeling that maybe I was not exactly where God needed me to be. Again at the urging of friends across the state, I applied for another prominent church in North Carolina. Just as before, the decision came down to me and they chose another minister. I returned to my work in Pelham again, but for the first time I was beginning to wonder if Pelham would be the only context in which I would do ministry. I thought I could be fine with that and I was taking these two failed attempts to move to other churches as a sign that I would spend my entire career in Caswell County. That was not a bad prospect to me. I was totally happy and had no real opposition or problems in my current ministry. I had achieved much and was a recognizable figure in Baptist life in North Carolina. What I was afraid of was that I was much too "at ease in Zion."

What I failed to see with the two attempts at a new pastorate was that my calling has not been to ministry situations that are doing well. Though I did not know it then, I now know that I am much better suited to fix something that is broken than I am to maintain that which is going well. I have come to think of my ministry as a ministry to brokenness. Repair and restoration are part and parcel of what I do best. The problem with my two attempts to leave Pelham is that each church was doing well and had strong ministries. These have not been the places that God has needed me. As I look back on almost four decades in ministry, I see that my assignments have not been plum assignments where I simply had to build on whatever is there. I have had to build from the ground up.

On Christmas Day 1997, I wrote two letters: one was a letter of resignation addressed to Shady Grove Baptist Church in Pelham and the other was a letter accepting the pastorate of Temple Memorial Baptist Church in High Point. Shady Grove was doing fine and may have been at her zenith. Things had taken a turn for the worse at Temple Memorial and she may have been at her lowest point. That sense of peace and calm that has characterized my knowing and doing God's will was strongly felt that Christmas Day. I would be sad about leaving the people and the place I loved so much, but I was sure that God wanted me where I was going. I was happy that God needed me and, where He needed me, I would go.

Lessons for Ministry:

1. God is always calling us to be. What we are to be may be radically different person to person. Praying about and meditating on what God wants you to be is good practice for discovering what it is that God wants you to do. If he calls you to be kind, patient and helpful, you will quickly discover opportunities to do ministry that incorporates what you have become. Seek to develop those things on your "to be" list.

2. God spends a long time getting us ready to do the ministry that he wants us to do. One's first place in ministry may be as much

a learning opportunity as it is a doing opportunity. Do not be too caught up in achieving preset goals as you are focused on developing who you are as a person and a minister and a leader. In turn, your gift of being who you are will help you to develop the best in other people.

3. Love people fiercely. Love the ones who love you and love the ones who don't love you. Love your work and love the place where you work. Love life and your place in life. Love God passionately. This comprehensive kind of love will cover a multitude of shortcomings – shortcomings in you and shortcomings in the people that you serve.

4. The circumstances that bring you to a place of service may not be what you expected. God is very able to work in ways that we did not expect. Brace yourself that God may come to you in a way that you least expect.

5. The most valued result of a loving and caring ministry is trust. Guard the trust that people have in you jealously. If it slips away, you may not be able to get it back. If you are fortunate enough to get it back after having lost it, it will not shine as brightly. Try not to lose it in the first place.

CHAPTER 12

"... THROUGH HIGH POINT ..."

I RECEIVED A CALL from a very kind woman who had been on the pastoral search committee when I failed to receive the call to Temple Memorial Baptist Church in High Point. I had not really kept up with the church over the years. That was partly because I was so deeply involved in my own work in Pelham and partly because I felt that there was no need to cry over spilled milk. They had chosen another minister and I had wished them well. This phone call came as a surprise. She told me that Temple was without a pastor (I knew this) and that she and other members of the pastoral search committee thought that I should consider becoming a candidate (I did not know this). I was sincerely not interested in pursuing Temple Memorial as things were going quite well for me in Pelham. But I must admit that a small portion of me was inclined to puff up: they didn't want me then, why would I want them now? I politely declined and ended the conversation feeling exceptionally good about myself. The kind lady did not give up.

Persistence pays off and she wore me down. I decided to send a resume' which was quickly met with an invitation to preach in early July 1997. The visit was a very pleasant one. I remembered the attendance was not as strong as it had been seven years earlier when I was a candidate for the church. But the kind reception that I received was the same as it had been before. I enjoyed preaching and they seemed to have enjoyed my preaching. On the drive back to Pelham, I kept toying with the idea of what it would be like to have an urban ministry. All the inevitable comparisons between Pelham and High Point, between urban and rural kept flashing in and out of my mind. I began to realize that I had most likely reached my zenith in Pelham. There were few giants left for me to slay. After seventeen years, I had accomplished more than I ever thought that I would. I still loved the good people of Shady Grove Baptist Church immensely, but I was becoming very interested in the members of the Temple Memorial Baptist Church.

The weeks following my July visit can only be described as a fully coordinated plan of attack to persuade me to pursue the Temple Memorial pastorate. I received multiple calls each week from various members of the search committee and those members apparently shared my contact information with other influential members. While I was being wooed by a segment of the search committee, I was also quietly making inquiries about the church. I was surprised to learn that many of the ministers who had encouraged me to apply following Dr. Macon's death now had a different feeling. According to them, the church had been badly damaged and was only a shadow of what it had been. My advisors advised me against going to Temple Memorial. Something better would come along if I just patiently waited.

My prayer life had become quite full with petitions to God to tell me if He wanted me at Temple Memorial or not. I think that we are sometimes prone to want to push the hard decisions of life onto God. If we can discover and discern His will and intent then we can spare ourselves that hard work of seeking after God, searching the Scriptures and of intensifying our own prayer life. I have found it true, more often than not, that God honors our hard work in the spiritual disciplines with both peace and purpose. While trying to discover whether God wanted me to turn left or right at this crossroad in my ministry, I came to understand – as had been the case countless times in my ministry – that God's claim on my life is not connected to the place where I am nor the condition that I am in. He can and does use me despite of those things. I came to the peace and calm of knowing that God would continue to use me if I remained in Pelham and He would use me if I moved on to High Point. A different zip code would not change anything about God's claim on my life to be His instrument.

With that calm, I began to weigh my decision in light of where I was needed. I knew that I was needed in the work that I was doing in Pelham, but I had this growing sense that I was needed more in High Point. I became energized by the thought of being an agent of God's love and grace and restoration for a church that was in decline. I decided that I wanted to be used by God in the "weary land" of High Point just as he was currently using me in the "green pastures and still waters" that Pelham had become. I wanted to be used by God. With that, I entered the pastoral search process in total. The search process had significant flaws and it was a long, hard and difficult process. I had several meetings during the months that it took the church to extend a call. The purpose of the many meetings was never really explained to me. I am not convinced that they knew why there was a need for so many redundant meetings either. The same questions routinely came up each time as well as questions that really had no connection to a pastoral search. I met with the search committee. I met with the deacons. I met with the joint board. I kept on meeting and meeting and meeting. I came to understand that there were differing factions at play behind the scene and I was simply caught in the middle of their tug of war. It was not as much about me as a person, but it was a struggle over what the office of pastor should really be about.

There were those who felt themselves to be the defenders of the congregation. They were determined that the next pastor would not have the means nor the authority to hurt the congregation as had been done with the last pastor. There was another faction that, due to the misdeeds of my predecessor, wanted a weak pastoral office and thought that the real leadership of the church should be in its officers. There were others still who were simply disillusioned by the role of pastor and saw the next pastor – whomever that was – as just more of the same. They were indifferent to me and just saw the call of the pastor as a necessary, unpleasant thing that the church had to do. And then there were those who came with their broken hearts and spirits in their hands wanting the next pastor to be the healer of their hurts, but who could not hide their anger at having given their trust and confidence to a pastor and who had squandered the precious gift that they had innocently offered. All these competing factions had one thing in common: they all had a strong passion for their church and, regardless of all that Temple Memorial had endured, they were determined to see better days for their beloved church. They just had no clue as to how they could roll the dark clouds away.

It took nearly six months from my first sermon in the summer of 1997 until the day that the church held a vote to extend a call to me. The vote was clearly in my favor, but there was a large contingent voting against my candidacy. I knew not to take that personally. I knew it was their reasonable uncertainty about calling any person to the church that they so loved. I am convinced that no candidate could have perfectly united the congregation on the choice of the next pastor. I was grateful to whatever majority the vote had managed to produce for me.

For some reason, I had given no thought at all to the idea that I might actually have to resign from Shady Grove. I didn't have a clue about how to actually resign. A panic came over me when I received the telephone call from Temple Memorial telling me that I had been elected their next pastor. It came on a Sunday afternoon. After the two morning worship services were over at Shady Grove, I remained alone in my office to wait for a call from High Point. I knew that the congregation would be voting after their worship service and I just wanted to be available if a call came. After the call came, I was in no way prepared on the best way to exit my current church. I wanted to let Shady Grove know as quickly as possible because I feared that the news might reach the members before I had a chance to tell them. I wanted them to hear it from me. So I actually spent Christmas Day writing two letters: one was my letter of acceptance to Temple Memorial and the other was my letter of resignation to Shady Grove. The letter to Temple Memorial was easy to write. The letter to Shady Grove took much more effort and required dozens of drafts and tweaks. I struggled to find the right way to say "I love you, but I am leaving you." Between every draft of the resignation letter, my mind would flood with the remembrances of the past seventeen years. I relived the joys of the accomplishments and I felt the pain of the struggles that I had shared with the members. It would be wrong to say that I did not have misgivings about my decision to even pursue the Temple Memorial pastorate. Shady Grove had been the place that I grew up – both as a minister and as a man. It would be hard to say goodbye. My second thoughts were coming in hurricane proportion. But I had come too far in the process to forsake the path now.

I moved from my home to the church around midday on Christmas Day. I needed the sacred quiet of an empty church to find the right words and phrases. After a couple of hours, I typed it on the church letterhead that never carried my name and signed it with a fountain pen. I took it to the empty sanctuary and found a familiar place on the front pew where I often came to gather my thoughts and pray. Through teary eyes, I prayed first for the members of Shady Grove and then for the members of Temple Memorial. I begged God for the wisdom to handle the coming days as I had handled the previous years. With the final "amen" said with trembling voice, I wiped my teary eyes and slid the letter of resignation under the paraments that covered the communion table. There the letter would hide – soaking up the holy purpose that the communion table represents – until the next Sunday morning when

I arrived just after dawn, retrieved it and put it in the breast pocket of my suit. I would offer my resignation after communion service on that Sunday. I had planned a special communion service to commemorate the last Sunday of the year. After recalling the words of Jesus telling His disciples that He would be leaving them, I told the good people of Shady Grove that I would be leaving them. I had intentionally made the communion services at Shady Grove a special time and I always gave very special attention to the words and atmosphere for communion. While it had always been solemn during my seventeen years, this was the first time it had been sad.

I sincerely wish that I had talked to the senior pastors who had been my friends about how best to transition from one pastorate to another. I made the very unwise choice to take three months to complete the transition. In the first month, there would be nothing other than the ordinary. I would fulfill my duties at Shady Grove as I always did. In month two, my duties would be split. I would preach at Temple for two Sundays and at Shady Grove for two Sundays. During the second month, I would also travel to High Point for even more meetings with officers and group leaders. During the last month, I would preach at Temple Memorial and come to Pelham a day or so in the week to finish up matters. I sent a minister friend of mine, Rev. Gary L. Cobb, to Temple Memorial to preach on the final Sunday of the three-month transition while I returned to Pelham to preach my final sermon as pastor of Shady Grove Baptist Church on Sunday, March 29, 1998. The transition period and plan were far too long and complex. It was hard – hard for me, hard for the church I was leaving and hard for the church that was anticipating my coming. I wish I had sought advice from other ministers and I wish I had not drawn the inevitable out for so long. It was painful for Shady Grove and I made a poor decision in making the new church wait so long.

What the three-month transition did was uncover all the details that were not disclosed to me during the six-month courtship. Temple Memorial was in much worse shape than I was told. I do not blame anyone for being intentionally deceptive. They were simply putting the best light on the situation in order to interest and attract a good minister to lead them. The former pastor had published an Annual Report which gave the membership to be nearly 1,000, the annual budget to be $750,000.00 and weekly attendance exceeding 600 people. None of that was true. About two hundred people were actually attending each week. Less than $200,000.00 was being raised for the annual budget. Much less was actually in the bank. My predecessor had been a master of deception and putting a good face on things. His paperwork was all that the committee had to share with me and it was quite misleading.

There were very high feelings of anger and utter disappointment in the congregation. Though the anger was not directed at me personally, some of it came my way because the congregation was angry at the former pastor. My predecessor had taken advantage of the congregation in many ways and, after his ouster, many improprieties had surfaced. There were evidences and rumors abounding that ranged from mismanagement to deception to theft. Truth and fantasy became so intertwined that I often did not know what to believe. The most devastating was claims of inappropriate behavior with some of the youth in the church. These charges ultimately led to a criminal conviction and time in the penal system. This recent history hung like a thick fog that encompassed everything. This history kept coming up in casual conversations with members and in meetings with leaders and groups. I was careful not to encourage a constant looking back, but I knew that a lot of people just needed to vent. I had to hear the same stories over and over again. Every time, I had to be empathetic with their feelings of hurt or anger or disappointment while being optimistic about the future. It drained me emotionally. Just like I had to search for something to unify my first congregation in my early days there, I found that my second congregation was already unified around one issue: we will never be taken advantage of again and, to be sure, we will guard our hearts, our pocketbooks, and our families from this new preacher.

I chose to devote my early weeks to preaching. By this time in my ministry, I had distinguished myself as a competent preacher and pastor. I knew that it would take a while for the church to embrace me as a good pastor, but it would not take as long to be embraced as a good preacher. As I had done in my early days at Shady Grove, I turned my preaching attention to New Testament themes of love, grace, forgiveness and hope – especially hope. While my preaching at Shady Grove had its greatest emphasis in the body (or points) of the sermon, I was very focused on the celebration (or closing) portion of the sermons at Temple. It was simple. A people who feel hurt and abused need something to celebrate. Temple's music ministry was superb and the choirs all performed well. Good music coupled with good preaching quickly produced an environment where people could release their anxiety and renew their hope for the future. While I spent Sundays offering uplift and hope, the rest of the week was spent trying to figure out how deep was the mess into which I had fallen. By every measure, it was very, very deep.

Pastoring people who live in the country was very different from pastoring people who live in the city. My pastoral style and emphasis changed dramatically at Temple Memorial from what they had been at Shady Grove. At Shady Grove, I spent most of my days away from the church office – visiting members at home or in the hospital, being present at schools, and being visible in the community. The members of Shady Grove saw these things as evidence of my being on the job. At Temple Memorial, there was a high expectation that I would be found at the Church. To them, a sign of a working pastor was connected to how much he was at the Church. Another distinction was with home visitation. In the country, people welcomed and looked forward to the pastor just dropping by. In the city, this was greatly discouraged. It was okay when a family invited the minister in for Sunday dinner or the like, but just visiting for no reason was thought to be strange. For a pastor who had come to love just "hanging out" with his members, the first months at Temple Memorial were quite lonely. I knew I would have to figure out my new church and understand my new members in order to determine exactly how best to serve and lead them. In this regard, I had a secret weapon and her name was Daisy.

Daisy M. Gregory was a legendary figure in the life of Temple Memorial Baptist Church. Her career as Church Clerk spanned nearly four decades. She had held the position through several pastoral administrations. When I arrived in early 1998 as Temple Memorial's pastor, Mrs. Gregory was prepared to monitor my administration as she had done with those ministers who served before me. Monitor was a good way to put it because it appeared that Mrs. Gregory's eyes and ears where everywhere. She knew all things Temple Memorial. Over the years, she had amassed a large presence in the life of the congregation. She was the center of church administration. It was to Mrs. Gregory that people interested in using the church for weddings, funerals or family gatherings came. It was to Mrs. Gregory that auxiliary leaders came for permission to have programs or have dates put on the church calendar. It was to Mrs. Gregory that employees of the church came to receive pay checks. It was to Mrs. Gregory that Trustees came to get permission to call plumbers, purchase light bulbs or change the landscaping. To say that Mrs. Gregory was the epicenter of the operation of the church would not have been an understatement. The trail to her office was the well-worn path that led to getting things done at 1458 Cedrow Drive.

Much worse than having to come to Mrs. Gregory for permission for this, that or the other was being summoned to her office for instruction, correction or rebuke. Her office often seemed like the principal's office at middle school whenever some member would be called to appear before Mrs. Gregory to explain their behavior in or out of church. I was amazed at the amount of influence that she had gained and the admiration that she had cultivated over the years. It was widely believed that had Mrs. Gregory not kept the church's checkbook in her personal possession the previous administration might actually have bankrupted the church. Her son served as Minister of Music at the church and the joyful sounds of the Voices of Temple had kept the congregation together during its most recent turmoil. The deacons regularly came to Mrs. Gregory for advice and inspiration as she was a matronly figure that they respected. The Trustees depended on her to review, revise and re-visit their decisions about the temporal matters of the church. Anyone who would become leader of Temple Memorial would have to deal with Daisy M. Gregory.

I was blessed because Daisy M. Gregory loved good pastors and she adored good preaching. She thought that both attributes were present in my coming to Temple Memorial. Almost every Monday morning was spent with her praise for the sermon of Sunday past. When I disagreed with her about the quality of my sermon, a strange look of bewilderment would come upon her face followed by a pitiful sad look as if to say, "Poor thing doesn't know how good he is." I brought a kitchen dinette set into my office in lieu of the traditional conference table. Almost every day, Mrs. Gregory and I would have lunch together there. She would command lunch from the day care center down the hall or bring something from home or call some member and pronounce what shalt be cooked and delivered for the pastor's and her lunch today. It was during these daily luncheons that the long history of Temple Memorial was unfolded to me. She informed me of the good, the bad and the ugly. Often they were all rolled up in the same person. It was not uncommon for her to become teary-eyed when recalling hard times for the church and she laughed heartily when telling the stories of the church's joy and accomplishment. Mrs. Gregory was prone to share only those pieces of information that somehow she knew I needed to know about the church, its members and the community that it served. She was never gossipy and she never told me more than she thought I needed to know. I had to often times press her for more information when she thought she had said enough. She was an excellent background provider. When a member of the congregation or a person in the community made an appointment to see me, I could expect a verbal dossier at lunch the day before. She was usually right on target and could often predict the nature of the meeting with amazing accuracy. When I showed a person to the door after concluding a meeting, I would find Mrs. Gregory laying back in her office chair at her desk with arms crossed and an expression on her face that clearly said "I told you so."

Mrs. Gregory saw her role as "protector" of the pastor. She literally screened calls to my office and decided who would and who would not be favored with an appointment to see me. If an unfamiliar female voice called the office, she would matter-of-factly ask what the strange voice wanted to talk to me about. If the response was not satisfactory to her, the caller would be informed that I was out of the office when I was literally sitting fifteen feet away from her desk. If a female appointee stayed too long in my office (where the door was always partly open according to her instructions), she would begin to have a coughing "fit" to let me know that whoever it was in the "much too short dress" had stayed too long.

I quickly came to adore Mrs. Gregory. I knew that she had offered her trust and confidence and that was a sacred offering that I knew I could never violate. She wanted me to do well at Temple Memorial because she wanted, more than anything else, Temple Memorial to do well. Like so many of the members, the Church was at the heart of their universes. They wanted the ugly stain that had been left on the church to be washed whiter than snow and they were expecting me to pull up my sleeves and get to scrubbing. One of the saddest days in my life was the day that I stood before a standing room only crowd in our 600-seat sanctuary to deliver the eulogy for Daisy M. Gregory. I knew I had lost a friend and a defender the likes of which I would never see again.

If Mrs. Gregory was a mother-protector figure for me, Robert F. Davis was my big brother and best friend. Bobby D (as he was known at church and in community) assumed the office of chairman of the deacons a year or so after my arrival. My early relationship with the first deacon chair I inherited had been at times strained. It was difficult for he and I to see things eye-to-eye. Even though it never spilled over into acrimony, I never felt that we were on the same team. Bobby D was totally different. Bobby D understood the pastoral role better than most. His grandfather, the late Dr. Fisher R. Mason, had been a pastor at Temple Memorial during Bobby D's youth and young adulthood. Dr. Mason spent much time with his young grandson and instilled in him certain values and gave Bobby D an understanding of the pastorate that is very rare among laypeople.

Bobby D had a great sense of humor and being around him was always fun. We took to joining forces several times a week to visit the sick and shut-ins in our church. That often was the high point of my week because hanging out with Bobby D was such a good release. Being with him was like having a mini-vacation while still on the job. Of course, we got some serious business of pastoral care in as well, but a week without time with Bobby D was always a hard week for me. Bobby D was generous in sharing the euphemisms and proverbs that his grandfather had told to him. His stories of his grandfather's ministry were often back-breaking hilarious, but they were so instructive to me. Those retellings helped me to understand a lot about being a pastor even though I'd already had seventeen years of experience by the time I arrived at Temple Memorial.

Another characteristic that Dr. Mason had instilled in his grandson was the language and the spirit of prayer. I loved to hear Bobby D pray. His talks with God so reminded me of the prayers that I heard from the deacons of my youth. His prayers were not performances (as was the case with some of our deacons) nor were their contrived utterances aimed more at getting the attention of the people instead of bringing the people into God's presence (as was the case with some of our deacons.) Bobby D's prayers were heartfelt pleadings for the presence and guidance of God in all things. He had a habit of calling my full name in his prayers. He would ask God to "bless Haywood T, Gray" instead of merely asking God to bless the pastor as an afterthought when he prayed. I always received his prayers as asking God to bless me in my whole personhood and not just in my role as pastor. His friendship blessed me; his sense of humor sustained me; his prayers strengthened me.

After Mrs. Gregory's passing, Bobby D and I conspired to get Joyce Baskins named to the Trustee Board of the church and as the Church Treasurer. Joyce was a wonderfully pleasant person who had had a long career in banking and corporate leadership. She was one of the most sincere Christians that I knew, but she was quiet about her strong faith. She enjoyed my good sermons (and told me so) and she felt sorry for me when my sermons were bad (and she told me so). Joyce's house was one of only a few homes that I frequented without invitation and we could talk for hours about more than Church stuff. She was such a pleasant person in every way.

However, Joyce was fierce in her role as Treasurer/Trustee. After Mrs. Gregory's death, the task of writing checks fell to me. Mrs. Gregory had kept the church's books for so many years that no one else literally knew how to handle that part of the church's administration. I computerized the process and instituted a voucher system to provide substantiation for every check written. Every week, I would prepare the checks and vouchers for Joyce's signature. She brought to bear every ounce of what she knew about corporate procedures, banking and commonsense. She let nothing get by and often saw small things that I missed. Her favorite thing was to say, "Rev., you really think I'm going to sign this? Where's the paperwork?"

I also contracted with my longtime personal accountant and the accountant who had done our audits at Shady Grove to work with us at Temple Memorial. The accountant and her assistant would make a monthly visit to High Point to review the books. I often thought that the accountants and Joyce were in league to make my life miserable. They let nothing slip by and it was not uncommon for me to have to re-do things that I had already done and submitted for review. In time, the list of recommendations from the accountants and Joyce became shorter and shorter. In time, I mastered the complexities of fiscal management. It goes without saying that what I learned being under the thumb of Joyce Baskins prepared me for what my next role would be after Temple Memorial. I was distressed to hear of Joyce's passing from a heart attack a few years ago. We had not kept in touch very much after I left High Point and I was sorry for that. I was even sorrier that I could not attend her funeral. I paused for some brief time during the hour of her funeral service to pray and thank God for her, for her friendship and for all the things she taught me about integrity, transparency and accountability. She was put in my path for a reason.

About midway of my tenure at Temple Memorial, I moved the church to an emphasis on missions. The concept and the idea was completely embraced by the congregation. To help me in that arena, I brought a good friend into the Church's employ as our first Director of Missions. Sandra Gant-Satterfield is truly the only woman I have known to have mastered so many things. San had a long and distinguished career in the social work profession. Our paths had crossed during my work in Caswell County when I was a pastor and school board member and she was directing a Head Start program in neighboring Alamance County.

San, like Bobby D, had been very close to her grandfather who was a stalwart Baptist deacon in Alamance County. San's faith was rock solid and she clearly had the legacy of her grandfather's faith. I trusted San's judgment and she trusted mine. We were a good team. San worked without my supervision and could take an idea or embrace a concept and develop a skeleton of an idea into an impressive outcome. She had a wonderful wit and let that side of her personality come through at the times that I needed it most. When challenges abounded in my ministry at Temple Memorial, twenty minutes in San's office rolled the dark clouds away.

Originally hired as a consultant for our day care program, San soon became our director of missions. In that role, she corralled the spiritual and physical energy of our congregation and extended the reach of our church globally. We became more connected to our local Baptist association and we became more consistent in our financial support for the objectives of our state convention. Delegates from our church began taking annual trips to the meetings of our foreign missions convention, Lott Carey Baptist Foreign Missionary Convention. However, the most remarkable part of her ministry as our director of missions was to lead each of our six missionary groups to take on making a meaningful difference in some local mission projects. By the time of my departure as Temple Memorial's pastor, the church was investing upwards of $150,000.00 of our $600,000.00 church budget to missions.

San's many talents were so helpful to our ministry. A professional counselor, she connected with many members who were uncomfortable bringing their cares to the pastor. A skilled writer, she could express the mission and meaning of our church in news releases and promotional materials to rival anything coming from Madison Avenue. A deeply spiritual person, she was able to help us uncover the biblical reasons for what we were doing and becoming as a church. She was also quick to point out when what we were doing had no biblical (or commonsense basis). San never minced her feelings with me: if I brought an idea to her that was silly, she said so. If it was an "ain't no way in the world" kind of idea, she let me know that. I respected her faith and her opinion that I always acquiesced to her opinion about my more outlandish ideas. However, when she thought that my "left field" ideas were important to me, she would spend days or weeks crafting something that would be better received and embraced by the congregation. Many of my pastoral ideas were saved, salvaged and improved by Sandra Gant-Satterfield.

Daisy M. Gregory. Robert F. Davis. Joyce Baskins. Sandra Gant-Satterfield. These were some of the people whom God used to "keep me on my feet" during my time at Temple Memorial. Without their support and their help, I am sure that I would never have been successful in High Point. All things considered, my time in High Point was a success. The church's public image was restored and she regained her place as a leading African-American congregation in the city. The membership grew considerably – first by members who had left during the previous storm returning and, then, by new members joining on a regular basis. The number of joining members increased so that I created a "Buddy Club" which was a personally selected group of members who were tasked with embracing, befriending and orienting new members immediately after their decision to join. With the fast growth of the church and the demands of church administration that had befallen me, it would often be weeks before I had the chance to meet with or get to know new members. The "Buddy Club" helped us not to lose new members by keeping them engaged until pastoral care and attention could be extended. Worship was rich at Temple Memorial and I often could not wait for Sunday to come. There was always an expectancy in the air about the sermon and the music beautifully accompanied what I was trying to achieve in preaching. The fellowship was warm and the house was always respectably full. The church prospered financially and, like at Pelham, I had been able to eliminate the church's debt which I inherited and build up considerable cash reserves for a "rainy day." The financial success was achieved even though we never had an overarching financial appeal each week. Nor did we engage in any gimmicks to increase revenues and we simply rarely did fundraisers. I truly believe that the financial support that the congregation realized came out of a deep sense of appreciation for the ministries of the church and a sincere and abiding love for Temple Memorial.

I found myself at home at Temple Memorial. The members learned to love me and I learned to love them. I admit that I was eyeing them suspiciously when I first arrived and they were doing the same to me. But when we got down to the business of the Church, we both discovered that both the congregation and their minister wanted to be faithful in serving God. The church had a large parsonage in a nice section of town and I used the parsonage as an extension of ministry. I often had groups over for meetings and meals. At one point, I cooked almost every weekend and had some people over on either Saturday afternoon or Sunday after church. While my predecessor did not allow visits at the parsonage from the members, I welcomed every chance that I could to have them over. It was a way for us to bond and build trust.

Because of the unfortunate circumstances that led my predecessor to a prison term, I was very careful about how I interacted with the youth of the church. I welcomed their affection at church and would greatly delight in a high five from a little person, but I was careful not to take too much time with any particular kids and never allowed young people to be alone in my presence. Our parents had nothing to worry about with me, but I knew that the image of the pastor alone with young people triggered some painful remembrances for some in the congregation. It was tough for me not to spend time in the day care center or to take carloads of kids out for ice cream or pizza as I had done in Pelham, but the wounds of the past were still tender and I needed to respect the caution that many parents felt. I remain convinced that had I been able to have the type of youth ministry I had in Pelham at Temple, I would have had a longer tenure than seven years. But there are times that one must do what it best for the faith community so that that community can continue to have faith even if it is not your personal heart's desire.

Instead of anchoring my ministry on youth as I had done in Pelham, I made young adults a major focus of my ministry emphasis. I concentrated on the late twenty-somethings and early thirty-somethings. In most cases, these were young marriages that were producing young families. For the most part, they had been ignored in the church prior to my coming. They were the most usual invitees to the parsonage for dinner or a grilling or just to "hang out." I helped them to confirm their faith and figure out how to live the life of Christ when most of their peers were outside the church. I helped them to navigate through the rough waters of marriage and counseled them when their young marriages fell apart. I constructed Bible studies specifically designed to meet them where they were on their life's journey. I became their advocate, their cheerleader, and their coach. I tried to help them mature in the faith. Working with young adults soon became the favorite and most rewarding part of my ministry at Temple Memorial. Some of these very young adults had promised themselves that they would never again set foot in a church building. Yet, before long, they never missed any event that threw open the doors of the church. I treasured the opportunity to see these young families grow in their faith. I know that ministry impacted their lives for the better and I felt a sense of fulfillment at helping them on their path. I do not intend to imply that their progress was even and always on the incline. There were stops and starts, faults and failings, disappointments and despair. But they never gave up on themselves and I never ever stopped believing in them.

Toward the end of my ministry in High Point, I began to see a trend that I had not seen before in ministry. Persons were joining our church in adulthood when they had no prior experience in the church. For most of my ministry career, young people had joined the church as youth and stayed until they reached young adulthood. Most strayed both from their faith and their raising, but many returned after a few years in the world. Though they had left for a while, they remembered the foundation that had been built from their childhood. On the contrary, I was finding that adults were joining our church who had never been in church as youth. As such, they did not always know the basics: how to act in church, what to do and what not to do, or the basic Bible stories that we learn from our young days in Sunday school. I found myself fielding questions from these new Christians about what this story or that allusion in my sermon meant. I found that the simplest matters of decorum in worship were unfamiliar to them. I realized that I was assuming that everybody was generally familiar with the stories of the Bible and the basics of "church," but I was discovering that this wasn't always the case. Now I was beginning to struggle with how wide the Bible knowledge span was between the generations in my congregation.

About the same time, I was beginning to feel the stress between the "traditional" worship style of the church and the call for a more "contemporary" worship style by the young adults who were flocking to our church. Most were being exposed to a variety of religious programming on cable television. Most had colleagues at work or friends from high school who were members of non-denominational churches. Some of them wanted their church to be more like others' churches were. I had solved this burgeoning problem in Pelham by instituting two worship services: the early service was contemporary in style and the morning service was very traditional in style. Neither I nor the congregation at Temple Memorial were interested in two services. I created a blended worship style that seems to satisfy both ends of the spectrum. I could not afford to alienate either end. If the traditional worshippers (who tended to be older members) were uncomfortable with the worship style, a problem would arise because they were the financial backbone for the ministry. If, on the other hand, the growing young adult component became unhappy with the worship, another problem would present itself. The young adults were the church's source for energy for missions and projects and service. Much of what we were doing as a church depended on their work and presence. It was a tightrope to walk, but I think we handled it well. The real difficulty was the struggle beginning in me.

In general, I was witnessing a transition in the African-American church. I saw the church that I loved and had served from youth changing. While it was not yet prominent in Temple Memorial, there was a tidal wave of change on the way. More and more churches were abandoning the traditional worship style and, with that, they were throwing out many of the valuable traditions that I held dear. Music in churches was being much more "feel good" and rarely either worshipful or theologically sound. Things like responsive readings and litanies that supported special occasions and themes were being abandoned. In an attempt to grow megachurches, some churches were becoming much more interested in attracting crowds than they were concerned about building lives and developing character. As a pastor, I knew the importance of innovation and creativity in ministry. I had used both as tools over the years, but I was beginning to feel that too many churches were trying to be "different" just for the sake of being different. There is, in my opinion, a huge gulf between being distinctive and being different. Being a church of distinction is hard work that must involve the people at every level and must birth ministries that are fit for the ills that face the people who are the church. Becoming a church of distinction takes time, requires talent, and demands nurturing. Simply being a different church requires only a new idea each week, or a new vision that supersedes the last vision, or simply the importing of something seen or done elsewhere.

I was afraid watching this coming change. I had known too many ministers who simply stayed too long. Their rich legacies of offering help and hope to people had dimmed because of an inability to assess when the time was right for transition in the church. I was looking for the signs and praying that I would be able to discern the signs when they appeared. I was growing paranoid that I might miss the indications that I had completed my assignment at Temple Memorial. I did not want to risk failing to realize when it was my time to move on to the next thing that God had in store for me. I thought that this sign had appeared when I was offered a job I could not refuse.

In my fifth year at Temple Memorial, my best friend who was pastoring one of North Carolina's fastest growing congregations, offered me a staff position at his church. I was already very familiar with the work and witness of this congregation. I had frequently preached for them. I had informally consulted with the pastor on ideas for fine tuning their already impressive ministry. I was comfortable with them and they were comfortable with me. I was ready to jump at the opportunity. I would be paid handsomely. I was assured that I would have the freedom to grow my area of ministry as I thought best. I would lead a church staff that was huge and experienced and dedicated. At last, I thought, I would have the "plum" assignment that had eluded me for most of my ministry. For once, I would not have to build something from the ground up, but I could actually be a part of something that was already established and headed in the right direction. For once, I would not be going into a church in crisis. I did far too little praying and far too much weighing of the pros and the cons. I really wanted to say yes, but I held out a little too long. Word began to leak that I was considering leaving High Point and I knew that I had to act quickly. I did not want the people I loved to hear this news in the lodge hall and in the barber shops and in the beauty salons. If it was to be told, I wanted them to hear it from me. I hastily called a meeting of the congregation after service one Sunday. That may have been one of the biggest mistakes in my entire pastoral ministry.

I was literally torn over what to do and even though I had called the congregation together, I was not sure what I really wanted to do nor what I really should do. Indecision from a leader is never a faith-inspiring thing. I really should not have involved the congregation until my heart was settled and my mind was made up. I was honest and told them that I had been offered another position and I admitted that I did not exactly know what I should do. The meeting immediately turned into a "you-can't-leave-us" kind of testimonial and I knew that I had made a mistake in involving their hearts in a place where my own heart was not sure. My detractors (few though they were) had new ammunition in their arsenal to try to convince other members of my being unfit to be pastor. But looming much more largely in my own head was the fact that I had let the people that I loved and for whom I deeply cared find such bitter disappointment in the idea that I wanted to leave. Leaving wasn't so much the issue as it was that I was unable to express why I was contemplating making so drastic a change in my life and career.

Looking back with some distance between that then and this now, I realize that there were several things at play. First, I was simply tired. I had never learned the discipline of self-care. I was prone to work hard and to work long. Vacations were few and, when they occurred, they were actually simply preaching assignments in some other pulpit than my own. I had worn myself down and instead of recognizing that as my problem I decided that leaving the senior pastor role was what I needed. Secondly, I needed the encouragement that I so easily offered to others. For most of my entire life, people had depended on me to help them make sense of their lives and to help them find smiles in the rubble of brokenness. This was a role that I enjoyed and a role that I knew was extremely important. However, there were times when I needed someone to encourage me. I needed someone to minister to me because my well of hope was drying up. In Pelham, I had a large circle of pastors who were friends. With them, I could be myself and talk "preacher talk." We were each other's mutual support. Finding that level of friendship and trust in High Point had been difficult. I had made friends with other pastors in town, but our dealings one with another were more professional than personal. For the most part, we did not hang out together, confide in each other or serve as each other's "leaning post." While I had a dozen or so close pastoral friends in Pelham, I had only one in High Point. Finally, I was very much reacting to a sense of frustration (or maybe it was disappointment) that my ministry was one that developed over the years in tough assignments. I had convinced myself that I was "owed" some ministry assignment that didn't require so much work physically, that didn't take so much from me emotionally, and that didn't need so much from me mentally. After almost twenty-five years in ministry, I had gotten puffed up and convinced myself that God owed me something for my faithfulness. I had cavalierly dismissed the reality that I owed Him everything. For the most part, I suffered little from my poorly thought out and even more poorly executed "exit plan" from Temple Memorial. The people were glad that I was staying. They forgave me for my faux pas and we continued on the good path that we had begun.

My detractors were a bit emboldened by my decision to stay. They finally had a legitimate gripe against me that they could use. I call them "detractors" instead of opposition because they never were really able to mount much of an opposition to my ministry in High Point. I must commend them, however, on their perseverance. Throughout my seven-year tenure, they were never able to convince more than a handful – seven or eight at their peak – that they had a near divine charge to point out my faults to the members of the Church. In their minds, the membership had been completely fooled by the good preaching, clean living, trusted service and complete dedication of the pastor. To them,

I had to be a fraud. Something just was not right with a preacher who acted like he was supposed to act, who didn't have favorites, and who was actually good at his job.

At one particularly hilarious point during my ministry at Temple Memorial, my detractors started having meetings to discuss "the pastor." A committee of seven dubbed themselves "The Eye Opening Committee" (because it was their job to "open the eyes" of the congregation). They published an anonymous letter that listed sixteen charges against my character and my reputation. Somehow they managed to get a copy of the Church's membership list and mailed envelopes (with no return address) to select members of the congregation. Their anonymity was questionable. Instead of signing their names to the petition, they listed their initials where full names should have gone. It did not occur to them to use fake initials to protect their privacy, but they used the actual letters of their first and last names. It took all of thirty seconds to figure out who the charter members of "The Eye Opening Committee" were.

To stimulate thought and discussion among the members, the sixteen complaints were given in the form of questions. Apparently, the committee members did not want to be accused of falsely accusing the very popular and effective pastor of anything, but if they posed the right questions, surely the congregation's eyes would come open. I kept a copy of the petition in my files for years. I referred to it often when some young pastor would come to me crying the blues over some minor matter (like his recommendation of the official church colors had been killed in debate.) I would show this young preacher who was in full "woe is me" mode that his issues could be much, much worse. I no longer remember what the complaints were in total, but I never forgot the question posed in petition #8: "Could it be that the pastor is on some kind of mood altering medication?" I found that especially funny as did most of the members whose mailboxes brought this "alarming" report from the "Eye Opening Committee." Some of the young adults would tease me after service and ask if I had taken "my meds" that Sunday.

All things considered, my days at Temple Memorial were good days. The church's self-image was repaired after having been shredded by the minister who preceded me. I left the church in a strong financial state with the mortgage burned and cash reserves well into six figures. I had assembled a competent staff and employees and volunteers who believed in the church's mission and vision. I had delighted in the tangible spiritual, social and personal growth that the young adults I mentored and inspired. Although my community involvement in High Point was only a shadow of the involvement I had had in Pelham, I did feel good about some matters of public life that our church influenced positive outcomes. Yet there was one goal that I set in my early days at Temple Memorial that I never realized. The goal of bringing the deacons of the church into a real partnership with me to do ministry never happened. While they did not prevent any ministry initiatives that I proposed, I never felt that I fully engaged them in the ministry as stakeholders and exemplars for the congregation. Lord knows, I tried.

I wish to emphasize here that there was no enmity between the deacons and me. I pretty much enjoyed being in their company at social gatherings and during informal chats with them one-on-one. Their handshakes were firm and sincere. They all could see the progress that the church had made. They, by in large, knew that the congregation was very satisfied with my service as pastor (except maybe for the members of the "Eye Opening Committee.") The church was strong, its ministries were growing, and the pastor's reputation about town was impeccable. However, these same deacons seemed to adopt a "group think" mentality whenever "two or three were gathered together." Meetings of the deacons became my great dread toward the end of my time in High Point. They would not be necessarily confrontational, but they were rarely helpful to enhancing our ministry as leaders of the church. Of the twelve men who served as deacons, not more than three of them really understood the office. Few had ever been trained for service and a few of them either forgot their training or never understood their training. I kept hoping that they would grow, but they never did. Some of them shrunk.

This matter had been partly my fault. Before coming to Temple Memorial, I was advised by the then deacon chairman that there were two men "on trial" to become deacons. These men had been selected after the previous pastor's departure and the deacon chair wanted to know if I might make their ordination a priority when I arrived. I was very frank and, because I had not been especially or favorably impressed with the deacons during my period of candidacy for the pastorate, I told him that I most certainly would not be ordaining deacons very soon. I told him that I was more interested in training the ones we already had. This deacon either convinced or connived the church into having these two men ordained before I arrived as pastor. Somehow the word got out that I would be a "deacon fighter" and a wall of mistrust was built between some of the deacons and their new pastor. I am not sure if this former deacon chair thought it was his personal duty to protect the deacons from this new pastor who would surely be getting rid of everybody or if he was trying to protect the church from the volcano that would erupt if I tried to remove the deacons wholesale. Neither was my intention, but the rumors and speculation persisted.

For the most part, the deacons took some of the blame for the indiscretions of my predecessor. The congregation blamed their leadership for allowing so many things to go on for so long. In reality, nothing that happened was truly the fault of the deacons. They, like the congregation, were beguiled by the craftiness of the person who was their pastor. When the anger from the members came to the surface, it was the deacons who took the brunt of the criticism and blame. They were determined to not be left holding the bag if I turned out to be another bad pastor. They thought themselves the watchdogs of the administration of church affairs and the protectors of the hearts of the people. The problem was that few of them were aware of what they should be watching for nor how they could protect themselves or anyone else. Over time, deacon meetings became their monthly opportunity to express their opinions (although their opinions were seldom on the issue under consideration), flex their muscles (when they rarely showed any leadership among the members), and complain about the performance of the pastor (which they became increasingly more adept at doing.).

The complaints that they voiced usually began with the statement that "I have been getting telephone calls about" or "all the talk in the street is." None of the complaints that were dutifully brought to the attention of the deacons was ever their own opinions, but it was what had been brought to their attention by concerned members. When asked (as I often did) who was complaining, the answer would always be very generic like "the people" or "the members." When I asked them what their recommendations would be to address the issue at hand, they rarely had any solutions to offer. Just complaints. If pressed hard enough, most of the complainers would finally admit that whatever they had brought into the discussion and consumed most of the meeting really wasn't anything to be worried about. I knew the source of these suggested "complaints" was no more than an opportunity for a complaining deacon to have "street cred." Nine out of ten times, the complaining deacon was expressing the feelings of a wife or immediate family member. When someone in a deacon's house was mad with me for something I did or for something I failed to do or for something that I would not let them do, I knew that I would have to be grilled on some totally unrelated matter at the next deacon's meeting. Over time, I became adept at accurately predicting which deacon would lead the complaining based on what deacon's wife or daughter or sister could not get her way. I didn't really take it to heart: I knew the brother had to go home after the meeting and report. When word got around among the other wives, daughters and sisters of the deacons that I had been chastised in deacons meeting, he would be a hero at home for a few weeks. It was much more of an irritation to me, but it gave a complaining deacon "street cred" at home.

It did not take me very long to determine the deficiencies in the deacon ministry when I arrived at Temple Memorial. I knew that they would not be very much help as a group to solve the problems that the church faced. So I spent more one-on-one time with the ones who showed some potential to become servant-leaders. I accomplished much more this way than was ever accomplished in group settings. I seriously considered ordaining new deacons and/or dismissing currently serving ones. I determined that either would have had disastrous results. The deacons in High Point's churches were very much a fraternity all their own. In many instances, the mere fact that a man was a deacon at Temple Memorial gave him status in the community and in the lodge hall. Most of the men valued that status much more than service. To have removed them would have surely created enemies for life. Even though most of them were very little help to me, I did not want them to become hindrances to me. I opted to let the wheat and the tares grow together. Because most of the deacons were held in low regard by the majority of the membership, it was difficult to get young adults with promise to become interested in studying for the diaconate. My best potential leaders among the laity did not want to be "one of them." The persons in the church who would have readily embraced the chance to join the deacon board were basically cut from the same cloth as the current deacons were. I seriously contemplated ordaining some women and making them deacons as I had done in Pelham, but the deacon board was rife with sexism. I intrinsically knew that this would be quite unfair to any female members to throw them into such a toxic mix. Not knowing exactly what to do, I did nothing.

After the disastrous way that I handled the offer to leave the church, the heretofore insignificant complaint sessions that I had to endure took a turn toward more biting criticism and near hostility. Instead of being just a segment of the meetings dedicated to hearing concerns, we had come to a place where we needed to call special meetings of the deacons with the sole purpose to hear complaints about the pastor and concerns about the church. Bobby D (who had become deacons chairman by then) always handled these meetings well. He was careful to remind the brethren of what their role was as a deacon and that we are a part of a spiritual organism. Before each meeting ended, Bobby D would give every deacon an opportunity to speak and voice his concerns. In most instances, Bobby D had already met with me to tell me what the big issues would be and allow me to get over any shock at the ridiculousness of the claim or get over the anger I felt at being the aim of frivolous complaints. Each time, I assured Bobby D that I would not say a word, that I would allow whatever tales to be told that were on the men's chests, and that I would not respond to any of the charges. After each meeting was over, I would go right back to doing the work I was doing as Temple Memorial's pastor. Both Bobby D and I agreed that nothing good would come from the agenda of the deacons spilling out into the congregation. By not confronting my accusers, we avoided larger confrontation that could have spilled over into the congregation. We always believed that whatever was being said would blow over after everyone had a chance to vent.

It worked well until one particular meeting night. The meeting was called to order as normal, Bobby D reminded the men of the spiritual nature of the meeting, and the floor was opened for "concerns." As usual, the complaints were minor and few. As usual before adjourning, Bobby D would go around the large conference table and ask each deacon if he had anything more to say or add before adjourning. Most of the time when we arrived at this point, everybody's heart and mind was clear. Apparently one of the deacons who rarely had anything to say had been either ridiculed or dared by one of his colleagues for his tendency to acquiesce toward the pastor. It was clear that his statement was not clearly thought out. As a matter of fact, he seemed startled to hear his name called with nothing of substance to add to the discussion. However, he aroused from his nearly asleep state and offered that "the people don't think you are doing a good job at preaching." A silence fell in the room and all eyes focused on the speaker. Bobby D asked him for clarification on the point he was making. He went on to suggest that, according to his sources —which, according also to him, were numerous – I had been a very good preacher when I started at Temple Memorial, but my preaching had become very bad in recent months. Bobby D broke the code of silence we had previously agreed upon and challenged the deacon on the point that he was making. Certainly Bobby D had heard nothing of the sort. One other deacon chimed in and basically dismissed this deacon's concern as a fantasy. But my accuser was adamant. My preaching had really gotten bad.

I think that I would have dismissed the discussion as that particular deacon feeling the pressure to think of something to complain about and nothing more. But the next thing that happened devastated me. Bobby D asked the remaining deacons if they had anything to say about what this particular brother had brought to the table. Only one other deacon rose to the defense of my preaching ministry and I was literally shocked. I am not suggesting that I am one of the world's greatest preachers – I am not and I likely will never be that. But I have always been very serious about preaching and I have worked hard at developing my craft. I was dismayed that such an outlandish claim would not be challenged by the other men in the room. Some of them had personally grown as men and as Christians under my preaching and we had discussed that often. Tonight they allowed the last word of the evening to be that my preaching skills were totally unsatisfactory to the congregation.

Through all of my life, deacons had been the agents of encouragement and growth for me. In my youth, the deacons of our little church in the backwoods of Virginia had taught me the skills of manhood and self-respect. When I was called to preach, it was to a deacon that my call was exposed and it was that deacon who first had faith in my report. In my early days of preaching, it was a deacon who drove me from preaching engagement to preaching engagement while constantly encouraging my tender heart in this new work. When I joined Calvary Church in college, it was the deacons who celebrated my growth in ministry and inquired about how I was managing ministry and college and life. At Shady Grove, it was the deacons who kept me encouraged, anticipated my needs, followed my leadership and stood like fortresses beside me as I grew from a twenty-year-old neophyte into one of the most prominent ministers and community leaders in the county. I had never really known deacons who did not seek to build up the ministry and the minister. I was surprised to have my preaching assaulted and only two of the twelve would defend my life's work.

The sign that I had been worried that I would miss for a few years now presented itself plainly in my view. I knew that this was the sign that I needed to see in order to begin my transition. I had done all that I needed to do in this place and I resolved that I would hop the next train coming through. That very night, while sitting in that conference room, I decided that I would complete one final task: eliminating the church's mortgage. After that goal, which was not very far in the distance, I would leave Temple Memorial and High Point. In my mind, the next place of service for me would be another church, maybe in the northeast or even perhaps the Midwest. I had no idea that the next train I would hop would lead me away from the pastorate and turn neither north nor west, but east to Raleigh, North Carolina.

Lessons for Ministry:

1. Just as God sends mentors, he also sends help. No minister can accomplish it all without assistance. God specializes in placing the right people in your circle who can help you achieve what God has planned for you. Do not feel threatened by people with skill and ability. They can be your ally in accomplishing God's plan for you. Welcome their skills and let their strengths sharpen your gifts.

2. People bring their baggage to church. Sometimes it is baggage from a failed relationship, a great disappointment or an incident (or accident) from their youthful days. No minister will be able to have everyone abandon the baggage that they have carried for years after one sermon, one prayer, or one counseling session. It may literally take years. But the minister can help them unpack their pain, one garment at a time. Having people wear just one less garment of shame or anger or disappointment is a significant accomplishment and should not be minimalized.

3. It is tricky business knowing exactly when a minister should leave one place of service and begin another. Simply being unhappy or feeling personally unfulfilled is not always the best measure. A better measure may come after a serious assessment of what you have accomplished, what has not been accomplished and an honest reality check about what can possibly yet be done. Ministry is not always pleasant and it is not always a happy place. However, it should always be a productive place. Though the fruit of your labor may be measured in inches and not by miles, it is still valuable work – it is essential to the lives of the people who are touched by your ministry. It is work that is honored by the One Who called you and the One Who will ultimately reward you. Remember that.

4. Pastors are often caught in the pull and tug of institutional advancement over the personal growth and development of individual persons. The attractive lure of what comes with having a large congregation, an experienced staff, a large budget and local renown is always a concern. These things that are evidence of institutional growth and strength bring contentment for a moment. Ten or twenty years hence, no one will remember how much money you raised, how interactive your website was, and how often you were invited to be someone's revivalist somewhere. But they will remember you being present for a time of crisis, a eulogy you delivered that helped light a candle of faith in a dark night of despair, or a sermon you preached that altered the course of their future. Growing, protecting and advancing the church as an institution is important. But sustaining the faith, enriching the spirit and deepening the commitment of the people in your church are the lasting things.

CHAPTER 13

"... TO RALEIGH"

I WOKE UP EARLY on the morning of Monday, January 3, 2005. It had been my first night in my new home in Raleigh. I had made a pallet on the master bedroom floor because I arrived three days before my furniture did. The bright morning sun shone brightly through the clean, bright window which had yet to be draped, or curtained, or blinded. I could not help but remember how reminiscent my waking up on the floor after having slept on a hastily made pallet of a blanket and a pillow was. In my youth that had often be my lot for sleeping when cousins from the north invaded my grandmother's house for the annual summer visits. The adults needed the beds and the kids could claim their squatters' rights on the rug in the living room or on the floor of a bedroom. However, a universe of difference separated the sleeping pallets of my youth and that day. As a kid, I woke up as a young boy who had no responsibility save for playing with cousins who lived in exotic places and revel in their re-tellings of their day-to-day life in the big city. That January day, I woke as an adult who had the great responsibility of being the executive head of one of the most prominent African-American Baptist state conventions in the nation. Forty years and a countless number of experiences separated those two pallet risings and, once again, my life would never be the same.

Six weeks earlier, I had been in Raleigh at the Martin Street Baptist Church for a special called meeting of the Executive Committee of the General Baptist State Convention of North Carolina, Inc. The forty members of the Convention's Executive Committee hire the Convention's chief executive officer referred to as the Executive Secretary-Treasurer. Their responsibility was also to fire the Executive Secretary-Treasurer. They had done both in the same calendar year. The dismissal of the previous Executive had been shoddily handled and had touched some very raw nerves across the state. The choice of finding a replacement had taken too long and wounds had festered into infections. The Convention was not well by any reasonable measure of good health. I had been informed that the Personnel Committee would recommend my name to the larger Committee and it was widely believed that I would win a majority of the members voting. But I was nervous and terribly unsettled. Things were moving at the speed of light it occurred to me. I had come into the mix rather late in the process. I formally applied for the position in mid-September. I had my principal interview for the job during the last week of October. Two weeks later, I found myself pacing back and forth in the parking lot of Martin Street Church waiting for the deliberations to close on the inside and hoping that the predictions of my friends would be true: I hoped to become the tenth Executive Secretary-Treasurer of the Convention I had previously served as an elected officer.

I was as close to being "all to pieces" as I had ever been in my life. The peace and calm that usually accompanied my ministry decisions were hiding from me this time. I was very much at peace with knowing that I had finished my work at Temple Memorial and it was time for a new work for me. However, I could not seem to find that centering calm to know that leaving the pastorate was the right move. For the past twenty-four years, someone had called me pastor though the adjective that preceded that title ranged the full spectrum from bad to best ever.

I had been a pastor since I was twenty years old. Being a pastor was only the second of the two full-time jobs I had ever had in my life. At the end of the day, I was good at being a pastor, but it was the only thing that I really knew how to do. This denominational leadership role would be something entirely different. I had done all the mental gymnastics about the pros and cons and, on paper and in my mind, it looked like a good move; but I was now in the midst of complete withdrawal from certainty. I had a nagging suspicion that I should have pursued another church as my venue for serving God. This field, I feared, would be much too large for me.

The late Dr. J. C. Harris came outside frantically looking for me. I was supposed to wait in one of the offices off from the sanctuary. My nervousness was so bad that I was hoping a walk in the cool breezes of a bright autumn afternoon would help center my thoughts and calm my nerves. It did neither. I walked to my car a couple of times with keys in hand trying to plot a quick escape before the verdict came. When Dr. Harris spotted me, a large grin exploded on his face and I knew it had gone well. When we reached each other, he extended his hand and said, "We are waiting on you, Mr. Secretary." I was breathing normally for the first time in more than two hours. The ordeal of waiting was over. I was glad.

However, it had not occurred to me that I would need to prepare an acceptance speech. On the way to Raleigh for the meeting, I could not embrace the reality that I would be the next executive leader of the Convention. I didn't have the presence of mind to think of something good to say. There I stood before the familiar and friendly faces of people that I had shared a friendship over many years. They were my colleagues and my fellow pastors. Terror rose in me because I was no longer looking into the faces of friends, but into the faces of my employers. I don't remember a word I said. I remember no applause coming from them in response. I am sure that it was one of the least stellar public utterances of my entire ministry. To my great delight, there came the much needed congratulations and back slaps after the meeting adjourned.

The trip to Raleigh that day had been anxiety-filled and the trip back to High Point was no less riddled with a cascade of thoughts and questions spilling into my mind. I had resolved not to make the transition from High Point to Raleigh as long and complex as I had made my transition from Shady Grove to Temple Memorial. I told the Executive Committee that I would be in place on January 1, a mere six weeks from the date of the meeting. I had so much to do. I had to plan my departure from the church I was serving. I had to find a place to live in Raleigh. I had to pack the valuables and trash the frivolous residing with me in the very nice and very large parsonage I had lived in for the last seven years. I had to figure out what the heck I was going to do in a position I never thought I would have. The next few weeks would go at a frenetic pace. Although I was used to having my world flow at unnaturally fast speeds, this interim time would seem to surpass the norm by double or triple.

I do not think that the news that I was leaving Temple Memorial came as a great surprise. Seeing that my previous mishandling of an opportunity to leave was still fresh in the minds of most of the people, it was seen as inevitable. The Church sponsored a very nice banquet gala at the local University that was warm and affirming. There was the expected sadness on the faces of the members who sincerely hated the idea of my going. Even the members of the "Eye Opening Committee" found some good things to say about the last seven years that I had served as Pastor. The church's sadness was coupled with a strong anxiety about who the next pastor would be. I tried to help alleviate their apprehension by putting a pulpit search process in place before my departure. The process was skeletal and they were encouraged to adjust it and amend it as needed once it got into gear after the first of the year. I arranged to have some preachers fill the pulpit for six weeks after my last Sunday.

For the most part, the members knew that I wished nothing but the best for them and that I was trying to make their transition as smooth as possible. I made a promise that I kept without fail: I would always love them and appreciate them for all the good things that they had done for me, but I would not meddle in their affairs after my departure. I would never again be their pastor, but I wanted to always be their friend. I would not (and I did not) assume any pastoral role after leaving High Point. I rarely visited and I was very selective about receiving phone calls and messages. I really would have loved to have kept up and in touch with the members, but the truth is that I became so overwhelmed by my new charge that I never had the time to show very much of myself a friend to my former church.

In addition to the business of transitioning away from Temple Memorial, I was trying to transition into my new job. I spent at least two or three days each week in Raleigh at the Convention's office building, the Baptist Headquarters. It was a sensitive and somewhat tense environment. A very smart and capable young minister had been asked to serve as Interim Executive Secretary-Treasurer before I filled the position. By mutual agreement, he and I agreed that he would remain in the office until the end of 2004 and I would start on January 1, 2005. I asked to be allowed to interact with staff and spend some time at the Headquarters in order to learn about the current financial position and current challenges of the Convention. He graciously consented and offered his office as my own. I politely declined the use of his office and I tried to limit my interactions with the staff. I did not want to give the appearance that he was being pushed aside prematurely and I did not want the staff to confuse what the lines of authority were. What I was learning from being on the periphery of things was what everyone already knew: the Convention was in deep financial trouble and morale was at one of the lowest points it had ever been. By not actually being officially in office, I was careful not to press anyone too hard for anything. Some requests were quickly met and others were only partly met and at a very slow pace. I knew better than to press or to try to exert any authority that I did not rightly have. I used what I had to paint the best picture that I could. Though I did not have a clear picture by any means, but the outlines were beginning to take shape and it did not look good at all.

One of the meetings that happened in the interim was a meeting of a special committee of the Executive Committee that was tasked with setting my compensation. I was warmly welcomed and there was a genuine sense that everyone in the room wished me well. The mutually acknowledged problem was the fact that the Convention's financial resources were already stretched. No one was able to give actual numbers of available cash on hand, but it was clear that the budget numbers would need to be sharply reduced. The final salary package that was offered was more than $35,000.00 less than my compensation package had been in High Point. When adding the value of the various benefits and honoraria I had received as a pastor and preacher, I would make almost $50,000.00 less in Raleigh than in High Point. To say the least, this was very discouraging. I assume that the Committee read my facial expression and my body language and they quickly agreed that the salary package would be reviewed in six months and adjusted based on how the overall financial posture of the Convention was moving. I reluctantly agreed, but I really had little other choice. I had already resigned at Temple Memorial and I certainly could not go back now.

Our heads butted, not over the issue of salary, but on the issue of vacation. I insisted on coming on with a minimum of a month of annual leave. The Committee wanted to hold me to the Convention's general personnel policy that gave five days of vacation to employees with less than five years of service. I was adamant. They showed resolve. Unable to agree, we agreed to table the issue of leave until some later date. (It ultimately took eight years and three personnel committees to resolve this issue.) I am not sure why I fought the leave issue so fiercely. I knew in my heart that time off would be next to impossible for me because it had been rare throughout the entirety of my ministry. Knowing the hard work that was ahead of me, I knew I could not afford a month of vacation in my first years. I guessed it boiled down to wanting to feel that I was getting something out of this major transition in my career: I wouldn't be gaining in compensation; it would require more work than any other job had required of me; offering me higher status and professional prestige was questionable considering the turmoil that the Convention had recently endured. I needed to satisfy the carnal side of me that I was getting something good out of the move. I was desperate for something to reassure myself that I had not quite made a complete fool of myself.

Rising early on that first Monday of January in 2005 brought two goals to mind: first, I wanted to get into the details of the limited information that had been shared with me over the past six weeks and, second, I had to get a handle on the first event that the Convention would have on the following Friday night. The Annual Martin Luther King, Jr. Memorial Banquet would be held on Friday, January 9th and the planning of the event had been done by the interim executive who preceded me. I knew that I would not be comfortable until I knew the particulars. When I returned to that pallet in the master bedroom of my new home in Raleigh around 9:00 p.m. after my first day at work, I was in a totally different place emotionally and mentally. Fifteen hours earlier, I had awakened with anticipation and excitement about beginning a new phase of ministry. I came home that night defeated and deflated. What I had learned my first day was that the Convention was basically broke and on an express bus to bankruptcy. The staff had compiled a list of nineteen bank accounts and the combined total cash in them all was just over $7,500.00. The best figure that the staff could put on the Convention's debt was well in excess of $1,000,000.00, but no one was exactly sure. Adding another layer of disappointment to my first day on the job, the upcoming annual banquet was a financial disaster waiting to happen. While the programming aspect of the event was impeccably planned, the financial assumptions about the event were grossly overstated. Ticket sales were way below the breakeven point and the expenses were not very tightly controlled. That pallet that had started the day as my springboard for a new career had now become my prayer rug that night. I prayed feverishly for the Convention, for the staff and for the wisdom and discernment that I needed for the days to come. I fell asleep in my clothes that night. I was too weary of it all to muster the strength to undress. And that first day at work would not be my worst day at work that first week.

Day two began early as had the first day. After being at the office for about an hour, I could not help but notice that the finance officer's telephone extension was lit much more often than anyone else's extension in the building. I walked down the hallway to her small office and found her on the phone. When the conversation was done, I asked her about the volume of phone calls that came to her phone and she told me that they were creditors. Apparently someone called every day and sometimes several times a day to ask for money that the Convention did not have. In speaking with her, I saw the grave weariness on her face. Her face lit up when I told her that I would be happy to speak with some of the creditors to help take some of the weight off her shoulders. I regretted that decision before the day was ended. Most of the angry creditor calls started coming to me. They did not care about my being new at the job nor were they concerned about the internal chaos that the Convention was undergoing. They wanted – and many demanded – payment of their accounts that were thirty, sixty, and ninety or, in some instances, more than a year overdue. The only thing I knew to do was to promise to get back to them soon.

When the phone did not have an incoming call demanding money, I was on the phone making an outgoing call trying to raise money. I was very fortunate to have built a long relationship of many years with pastors and churches across the state. Having been in the Convention for nearly twenty-five years, I had made many friends in churches stretching from the mountains to the coast. I was calling everyone I knew and pleading for their support – as a friend and as a former pastoral colleague in the Convention – for the upcoming banquet. I really did not have a handle on the depth of the Convention's fiscal problems and I did not want to risk sounding more of an alarm than had already been heard across the state. I framed my appeal as a kind of "personal" favor to make the banquet (which would be the first event of my career as Executive Secretary-Treasurer) as successful as possible with high attendance. Practically every pastor I called agreed to either attend with their spouse and a good number even agreed to buy tickets and send members of their churches. I gave every one on the staff the same assignment to call anyone and everyone they had any kind of relationship and beg, plead or even cry to get these banquet tickets sold. Slowly the banquet's balance sheet was becoming less and less skewed. I read and re-read the contract looking for small items that could be eliminated to cut costs that might not be noticed by the attendees. But the phone calls threatening legal action if we did not pay our bills did not abate simply because my top priority of day two was raising money.

I was feeling better about things related to the upcoming banquet by day three of my first week, but my budding optimism was smashed into ten thousand tiny pieces on the afternoon of my third day at work. A deputy of the Wake County Sheriff's Department arrived with legal papers. The Convention was being sued. Another suitor for the job I had taken was suing the Convention claiming that a technicality made the meeting of November 15 invalid. According to the suit being filed, I was actually not Executive Secretary-Treasurer because the action was invalid. The suit sought my immediate removal from the job I had just begun, demanded certain changes to the Convention's Constitution regarding the position of Executive Secretary-Treasurer and requested $10,000.00 in damages to the party bringing the suit. I had been so consumed with the Convention's fiscal position for the past seventy-two hours that the only part of the suit that actually worried me was where we would get $10,000.00 if the suing party prevailed in court. It had not set in with me that if the party prevailed, I would be out of a job. I really thought that things could not get worse, but day four had not yet dawned.

I arranged to have breakfast with The Reverend Dr. Charles T. Bullock, the President of the Convention, at a popular downtown breakfast spot. This particular restaurant was the only really bright spot that I enjoyed in my early days in office. It was to this restaurant that I had come a few weeks earlier to meet with The Reverend Dr. David C. Forbes, Sr. Over scrambled eggs and link sausages, Dr. Forbes and I discussed the possibility of my becoming a member of the church that he then pastored. I had become obsessed with worry over the fact that, upon moving to Raleigh, I would not be affiliated with a church. This would be the first time in almost thirty-five years that I had not been affiliated with a church. That frightened me. Although I had resolved the internal conflict about not being a pastor again, I couldn't figure out what I would be doing on Sundays anymore. The words of the Baptist Church Covenant that I had memorized as a youth kept playing in an almost endless loop in my mind: *"We furthermore resolve that when we remove from this place, we shall, as soon as possible, unite with some other church where we may carry out the spirit of this covenant and the principles of God's word."* I did not want to move to Raleigh without having a church home. That was a covering that I desired and needed.

I had chosen to meet with Dr. Forbes to discuss the idea of becoming a member before taking the initiative to walk down the aisle of the

Christian Faith Baptist Church and respond to the Invitation to Discipleship. While I had never really seen it done, I was not exactly sure that I would be received into the membership of the church. The tone of my discussion with Dr. Forbes was rather in the "may I join your Church, pretty please?" mode. I knew that wherever I joined would bring a spotlight of scrutiny and I did not want to burden any pastor or church with undue conversation about how badly I may be doing in the top job. Likewise, I knew that whatever church I chose would be in for extra and largely underserved scrutiny. I was also aware that few people really believed that I would be able to stabilize the Convention. The odds were heavily favoring the possibility that I would be an utter failure and the individual who had been hired to baptize the Convention into a new era of service and strength might instead be its eulogist. I did not want my failure to bring any embarrassment upon a congregation that I might join.

Dr. Forbes quickly dismissed my "foolish assumptions." He expressed his confidence that I would do well in my new job and that I had his support. He assured me that I would have Christian Faith Baptist Church in my corner whether I decided to join or if I chose another church. He was genuinely excited about possibility of being the EST's pastor. Although we had been friends across the years, he convinced me that he would be happy and honored to assume the pastoral role and offer guidance where appropriate and prayers without ceasing. In some ways, I felt a tinge of what I felt a long time ago when as a child I had fallen into the outstretched arms of Reverend Raymond L. Lassiter, Sr. and joined his Church. It felt good, it felt right, to know that I would not be churchless in my new hometown of Raleigh, North Carolina. I breathed a sigh of relief and offered a "thank you, Jesus" that was silent on my lips, but was loud in my soul.

It was clear that I had not grasped what this new job and this large responsibility would be. I told Dr. Forbes that I wanted no special assignment or duty at the Church. I would be content to be a last row bench warmer. I told him I could not sing a lick and I had too many aches and pains to be an usher. The joke made us both laugh, but he responded that he would not put great responsibilities on me. He told me, in a near prophetic way, that I would rarely be at Christian Faith. He told me that I would be in great demand as a Sunday morning preacher, that I would travel the state for the greater part of most weeks, and I would be called upon to serve Baptist causes at meetings across the nation. I quietly thought he was off his rocker, but he proved to be absolutely on point in each prophecy. I left that breakfast meeting with my soon to be pastor feeling more confident about the new course my life was about to take. Now just two weeks hence, I had returned to that same restaurant and ordered the same breakfast that Dr. Forbes and I had shared. I wanted desperately to feel as good about my new job as I had felt at the end of the morning that I had spent with Dr. Forbes. But what a difference two weeks makes!

I met Dr. Bullock early on the fourth morning of my first week at Baptist Headquarters. I ordered the comfort food that I had come to so enjoy and we began to discuss a wide variety of things, the impending lawsuit at the top of the list. At the end of the discussion, Dr. Bullock had an additional conversation that he wanted to have with me. I had no idea what it could be. I braced for the worse and Dr. Bullock did not disappoint me.

The General Baptist State Convention was organized in 1867 around the purpose of raising funds among the Baptist Churches that were springing up all across the state following the Civil War to support a school for ministers and teachers that Dr. Henry Martin Tupper had started in Raleigh. The school would ultimately become Shaw University, the oldest historically black college in the southern United States. Over time, the Convention added other objectives to its raison d'etre. Lott Carey Baptist Foreign Missions Convention, the Central

Children's Home of North Carolina, Inc. and the J. J. Johnson Baptist Assembly joined Shaw University and Shaw Divinity School as the chief objectives for the Convention. In its one hundred fifty years of existence, the objectives and support for missions has been the unifying matter for Baptist Churches in North Carolina that are diverse in every measure. The Convention is a leading stakeholder in each of these partner organizations. The financial support, over the years, has been dependable and essential.

Unfortunately, in its struggle to survive, the Convention had become delinquent in passing along the funds that it had raised to the various agencies for which it was raised. By the time of my arrival, the Convention was in excess of $250,000.00 of debt to the objectives. The debate continues to this day as to how necessary it was for the Convention to use these funds for operations, but the Convention found no empathy from the objectives. Some had begun to press the Headquarters for the money owed to them. Because our support is so critical to their operation, President Bullock was regularly getting phone calls from agency heads alternately complaining about late payments and demanding that matters improve. One agency head had taken his case to the moderators of prominent associations and pastors across the state directly. His choice to take the matter in his own hands had a devastating effect. Many of our major donors lost confidence in the stability of the Headquarters and giving – on all levels – decreased significantly. Dr. Bullock expressed his very clear instruction to me that day. He wanted the objectives paid and he wanted them paid before any other bills. I was somewhat taken aback. Dr. Bullock had not been particularly forceful on matters in the many meetings we'd had prior to my moving in at Headquarters. His position had been that I needed time to chart a course and he was looking forward to hear my suggestions in due time. While I agreed with the President in principal, I was surprised to hear him frame it in terms of a mandate.

I agreed to look at how that could happen and promised to get back to him promptly.

I spent the rest of the day dodging calling creditors, finalizing plans for the banquet which would be held the following night and crunching numbers about how we could meet the President's mandate of paying the objectives first. I was drained of everything I had at the end of day four. I stayed at the Baptist Headquarters well past midnight on day four. What little optimism I had was completely gone. I was between the proverbial rock and a hard place. If I paid our creditors as I had been promising on the phone all week, there would not be enough money for the objectives. If I paid the objectives as the President wanted me to do, there would not be enough cash to make good on the promises I had made to our creditors. Looming just one week out was another crisis. Next Thursday would be my first payroll and there would not be enough money to pay the staff, pass along the objectives' money and make progress on the many companies that the Convention owed. The only immediate option would be for me to forgo collecting my salary in order to make sure that the staff would be paid and that the objectives would be satisfied. (As a matter of fact, I did not receive my first salary check until August 2005 – eight months after I began the job. Even though I cashed my payroll check on the 15th of August, I had to void the payroll check for the 30th of the month. It would be November before I could count on actually receiving my salary on a semi-regular basis.)

My financial forecasts from earlier in the day led me to another depressing conclusion. Because the Convention's credit had been virtually ruined for late payments, slow payments and no payments, it would be impossible to purchase the normal items necessary for day-to-day operation. I knew that my only option would be to use my personal credit for Convention business until things were better. (I ultimately did have to take out a personal loan for my personal living expenses while I was not collecting a paycheck. Similarly, I had to use my own personal credit cards to string along the day-to-day operational needs of the Convention. At one point, my personal credit card debt was more than $75,000.00 in Convention-related expenses with only honoraria from churches that invited me to preach as my only income.)

I have never shared what followed with anyone. I realize that I may have actually tried to forget it. The pain I was feeling at this time was so profound, so real, so overwhelming that I have purposely tried not to return to it. I have never shared these recollections for even when I have thought about them in times of reflection, I come to tears these many years hence. But I now understand that this entire book is written to tell this final story. This is what this book is really all about.

I sat at the desk in the office that was not fully unpacked. In four days, I had not had the time to get organized, to decorate or to completely unpack. I was defeated and I had not felt a hurt so persuasive before in my life. This bitter taste exceeded the humiliation of Mrs. Pope's fifth grade class and the despair of a birthday party that went wrong. This sense of failure and despair touched me at my core. I was too tired to sing a hymn, too weary to find solace in Scripture that I quoted frequently, and too worn out to pray. I had not had a good cry in a long time and the tears that came down my face were as if the valve on a pressure cooker had been released. I had this overwhelming sense of failure and fatigue and I could not determine if failure or fatigue was the bigger giant who had slain my hopes and dreams.

There was only one thing I thought to do. I would resign. I would save President Bullock and the Convention the further embarrassment of having employed a person so unfit and so unprepared for the task. I pulled myself together as best I could and I loaded the printer with letterhead that did not yet bear my name. I crafted a resignation letter that put the fault squarely on my ill-preparedness. In it, I asked for the

Convention's forgiveness that I had been so thoroughly unprepared for this job and so completely overwhelmed by the challenges that the job presented.

I did not have a communion table to leave that letter of resignation on as I had done with the letter I wrote when transitioning from Pelham to High Point. Instead I laid it face down on the great Seal of the Convention that is centered under the glass on the conference table in my office. I was hoping that my words of resignation would gain something from all that the Seal of the Convention represented. I had resolved to read the letter to the gathering that would happen on the next night to come at the Martin Luther King, Jr. Memorial Banquet. I told no one. I was too weary to even talk with God about it. My only prayer was that the error of hiring me would not further impede the work of this Convention that I loved. Also I could not think of anyone who would listen to my plan and not be disappointed. Finally, seeing that I was being sued for the position that I held anyway, I did not want my detractors to get wind that they had won before they had to know. In four days, I had failed miserably and I had only myself to blame for even getting in this mess.

Friday of that first week was more of the same. I spent the day fielding calls from creditors, making final preparations for the evening's event, and keeping my fingers crossed that the pastors and churches who promised to be there would come through. I left for home early that day. I had reserved a tuxedo for my first event as "Mr. Secretary" and I figured that I might as well go out in style. After getting ready for the gala event, I hurried back to the office, gathered papers necessary for the evening, and headed off to what would be my first and my last event as Executive Secretary-Treasurer of the General Baptist State Convention. The turnout was phenomenal. Almost 1,000 people had gathered in the Convention Center and the mood was unusually festive. There was a sense of optimism and hope in the air. I saw it on the faces of people, I felt it in the firm handshakes they generously offered and I sensed the genuineness of their embrace. Perhaps if I had not been so physically and mentally exhausted from the previous four days, I too would have caught the spirit that was in the air. However, I had nothing more to give and there was nothing left in me that could be the growing field for optimism or celebration. I managed to smile and gave warm greetings and firm handshakes as well, but they were more from a coming sense of relief that I would soon be done with this unconquerable task.

The tradition of the Convention is to give the Executive Secretary-Treasurer a brief time to make remarks at the King Banquet. Inasmuch as the banquet is the first event of the calendar year, the EST's comments are highly anticipated. They often can set the tone for the coming year. Having heard more than a few speeches from the Executive Secretary-Treasurer over the past twenty years, I knew how important that moment was. In anticipation, I had crafted a speech long before I had moved to Raleigh. I had actually written the speech over the Thanksgiving holiday while still pastor at Temple Memorial. I wish that I had had something more thought out to say to the Executive Committee when I was hired. I did not want to be in that situation again so I wrote a brief homiletic that centered on the word "shall." My basic premise was that the extent that people can be successful in the ventures that they decide upon is always questionable. People might succeed. People might win. People possibly will come out the better. I contrasted that with the language of the Bible that always seemed to equate God not with the words of might, or maybe, or possibly, but always with the word "shall." The point of the speech was to be honest with the dire straits that the Convention was presently in, but to remind all of us that "with God all things are possible." Other matters claimed my attention over the next few weeks and I never returned to the task of finishing and polishing that script.

In the moments before my time to appear on stage came, I reached for the leather folder into which I had placed the letter of resignation I had written the night before. To my surprise, in my haste and indiscriminate gathering of the papers on the conference table in my office, I had mistakenly picked up the unfinished "shall" speech and not the resignation letter. My first thought was there could not be anything else that could possibly go wrong in my world. But I could not further embarrass myself or the Convention by not having something to say so I decided to go ahead with the basic parameters speech. I would simply inform the Convention leadership of my intention to resign after the Banquet. I would FedEx copies of the letter to the appropriate officials on Monday.

My new pastor, Dr. Forbes, had been given the task of introducing the new Executive Secretary-Treasurer to the gathered assembly. Dr. Forbes is a master wordsmith and was much too glowing and far too complimentary in his introduction and confidence. My new Church, which I had only attended once when I had joined the previous Sunday, sent a $3,000.00 contribution to commemorate and celebrate my new work. I was half listening to Dr. Forbes and reviewing the text (which was still incomplete) of the speech that I had written weeks earlier. I would have to read it from the page because so much had transpired since the time it was written and the time that it would be delivered. By now, I was wholly unfamiliar with it. I had not had the time to type it, but it was in my own handwriting on only a couple pages unevenly torn from a legal pad.

The text was in my handwriting, but it was becoming clear to me that they were not my words. The following words were written in the second or third paragraph of the speech: *"a strong wind forces some to retreat, to give up on their dreams, and to abandon their visions. But a select few -- instead of giving into their fears – lift their heads, square their shoulders, and challenge life's gale force winds."* The impact of those forty

223

words hit me with the force of forty tons. In a moment, in the twinkling of an eye, it all came together for me. A life changing revelation came to me that was as clear to me as had anything that I had known in my life. And the calm and peace that had eluded me since I had started the pursuit and process for this job came to me and into my spirit as if it were a rushing mighty wind. Though I had come to this calm assurance many times before in life and ministry, this was the first time that it had come accompanied by such a holy boldness.

What I realized in that moment was that I had not arrived at this place by accident. It was not merely the convergence of a long series of coincidences. I also intrinsically knew that I was not here by my own prowess or intelligence or machinations. My entire life had been guided by a Hand Unseen. Now in this holy moment, I could see how one experience prepared me for the next experience and that one for the one that followed. I understood how certain people had been sent my way to plant a seed or to water some other seed that had already been sown in my life by another. Suddenly I realized why certain mentors entered and exited my world on an unknown schedule, but with timing that was always quite precise. I could appreciate how the places I had served had each given me a small measure of the wisdom, fortitude and courage that I would need to be successful in this new ministry. And now I was sure that this same Unseen Hand had actually taken my own hand and penned the words that struck me so forcefully in this speech. The speech had not really been written for the large crowd that gathered; the speech had been written for me. I lifted my head, squared my shoulders, and resolved to withstand the strong winds that tried to press me into full retreat. I was completely uncertain as to what I would do to solve all the problems that had been presented during my first week on the job, but I was certain of one thing that I most certainly would not do: I would not quit!

I gripped the sides of that podium and I was confident with this sense of boldness and purpose that was coursing through my veins. I read the words that were on the page and the Spirit of a Living and Holy God began to move in that heretofore unremarkable room that had been somehow transformed into a sacred space. The written speech ended with the contrast between humanity's might's and God's shall's. The crowd's responses enlivened me. The preachers who rose to their feet emboldened me. The blessed assurance within me encouraged me. I felt better, so much better, since I laid my burdens down.

I closed the leather binder, but I opened my mouth. I reminded the gathering of the eternal truths from the sacred canon. *"They that wait upon the Lord **SHALL** renew their strength." "They shall be as a tree planted by the rivers of water and whatsoever they doeth **SHALL** prosper." "Behold, a virgin **SHALL** be with child, and **SHALL** bring forth a son, and they **SHALL** call his name Emmanuel." "Blessed are the pure in heart for they **SHALL** see God." "And God Himself **SHALL** be with them and be their God. And God **SHALL** wipe away all tears from their eyes."*

I am content to end this story there. There is little to be gained by telling more about the struggles and difficulties with which I have had to contend in the nearly twelve years that I have occupied the Office of Executive Secretary-Treasurer. That first week has replayed itself in some smaller measure throughout my entire tenure. I am happy to report that I have not since had a time of such intense pressure and hopelessness, but there have been pastel shades of those frightening colors from time to time.

The good news is that the Unseen Hand did not leave my life after I left the pastorate. I did eventually begin to draw a regular paycheck. The personal debt that I assumed to help move the Convention forward was ultimately repaid. The agencies that the Convention supports laid down their swords and have become loving partners in our Baptist enterprise in North Carolina. I have been the subject of several lawsuits, but I have prevailed in them all. The angry phone calls from unpaid creditors stopped coming in hurricane proportion. All of the debts – whether owed to a person, a company, an objective, an agency or a bank, all $2.9 million of it – have been repaid. The Convention satisfied its final debt with the close of the 2007-08 fiscal year and the Convention had operated debt free since August 31, 2008. Some of the persons who competed against me for this appointment have, over time, become dependable supporters and personal friends. The reputation of the Convention as a premier institution has been restored and its influence widened around the world. In my early days, the Convention's concerns and endorsement over public policy were intentionally avoided by political leaders and persons of influence across the state. Now these persons actively seek the blessing of our Baptist family in their circles of influence. Integrity, honesty, openness and transparency have become the hallmarks of the business affairs of the Convention. A feeling of confidence in the administration has taken root across the state. I take great delight in mentoring young pastors and an increasing number of college students. I am fortunate and blessed to be able to stamp the imprimatur of my view of ministry on the promising and budding ministries of young people who are under the umbrella of my influence and instruction. Life and ministry for me are good.

But I do not want to be unfair to history and suggest that there have not been some other low places in my more than twelve years in this position of honor and service. I have been subject to disloyalty on the part of former staff members who spent more time attempting to undermine my authority and damage my reputation than they spent on doing ministry. There have been seasons when some elected leaders have sought more from having position and power than they have been concerned about service and humility. An ever growing challenge has been trying to keep the children of the parent body on task and focused. Grown children, however, are notorious for rebelling against the principles of their upbringing. There have been trying times when there were threats and attempts to split the Convention or to separate from the parent body. I am glad to say that all of those efforts at division have fizzled. I regret that I have to spend far too much time massaging egos that have already grown to unhealthy proportions. I have often had to scramble to do crisis fundraising and begging for bread has become one of my professional strengths. This venue of service has not been easy. It has certainly been a struggle. The work of the Executive Secretary-Treasurer is characterized by long hours, hard work, brutal schedules, lonely travels, difficult decisions and sacrifice after sacrifice after sacrifice.

If I am very fortunate, I will be able to retire from this position. However, that is no certainty. I work at the pleasure of a committee of people who have ideas that sometime differ from my best advice about how to move the Convention forward. There is a high probability that I may not always have the favor of my employers that I currently enjoy. I am acutely aware of that and I try to stay mentally and financially prepared for that possibility. But I spend much more time pondering what to do to make the work more effective than I spend in trying to predict how much longer I have in the work.

Whatever is my fate for the next ten years, I am certain of one thing. Whatever I do, wherever I serve, whatever I am, I will have the blessed guidance of an Unseen Hand. I will trust that Unseen Hand to continue to set the stage upon which the drama that is my life is acted. It is that Unseen Hand that will continue to mark destinations and draw arrows on the road map that is the divine plan for my ministry. I have learned -- over many years and "through many dangers, toils and snares" – to trust this Unseen Hand. And when the last page of the book that is my life is written, I will expect that Unseen Hand to cradle my weary soul in its hallowed and hollowed palm and carry it away to a place called Paradise where one day there will be pay for every fear, every tear, every disappointment, every heartache and every headache here.

227

"Lessons for Ministry"

1. "To whom much is given, much is required." Do not forget that very important truth when you are petitioning God for a higher place and a large field of service. You may very well get what you have asked for, but will you be ready to pay what the desire of your heart costs?

2. While God calls us into the venue of service that He chooses, it is our obligation to manage our lives in such a way that we can be effective where God calls us to be. Since my youth, I have been a penny pincher. By the time that I arrived in Raleigh, I had built an excellent credit rating and had savings in reserve. God used those resources to move the Convention through a very rough period. It was my contribution and offering to God to have so ordered my affairs to have been able to offer my personal credit and financial resources. Watch your finances, take care of your business, and guard your reputation! You never know when God may need them.

3. Desperation may be the place where God has made a reservation to usher you into a feast where your soul will find nourishment and your spirit will drink from deep reservoir. Remember that you may not always receive an engraved invitation to these places of refreshment. It often may be a surprise party when you need it most.

SIMPLY GRATEFUL

A LMOST THREE YEARS marked the time between this book's genesis and its completion. Most of the work happened in remarkably quick order toward the end of that trio of years. Most of the months, it lay untouched in a nondescript file on the hard drive of my computer. The title was simply "The Book." I have come to believe that it was not a lack of ideas or any difficulty in putting my thoughts into credible expression that hindered my progress. In the beginning, I lacked the encouragement, support and correction of the right people to make this project a reality. Toward this end, God guided some other very important people to intersect with my life at the time of this writing and they deserve much credit for helping me to see this through to the end.

Primary among this class of helping persons is The Reverend April R. Rhinehardt. Rev. Rhinehardt is the University Chaplain for Shaw University in Raleigh, North Carolina. Shaw is the oldest HBCU in the southern United States. She had only been on the campus for only one academic year when I commandeered her time and instruction during the summer session when the Thomas J. Boyd Chapel was in summer recess. The time, talent and attention that she normally would have given to young college students became time to nurture, develop and guide the work that eventually became this book. She read and re-read the several versions of the manuscript and offered valuable suggestions for improvement and clarity. If there is anything good in these pages, a significant amount of credit goes to Rev. Rhinehardt for challenging me to dig in the fields of my life and ministry to find those pearls of great price. Initially, I was principally concerned with writing something that would help, inform and encourage others. Rev. Rhinehardt kept challenging me to find something for myself in these lessons and stories. At first, it seemed a strange request to make, but when the final pages came to life on my computer screen, I finally understood what Rev. Rhinehardt meant. I am grateful that she never relented in pressing me to find help and hope in my own words.

The Reverend Thomas R. Farrow, Jr. is pastor of the Reeder Memorial Baptist Church of Charlotte (North Carolina). This good Pastor is in his first year with that congregation. He came to my attention during his six years in the pastorate of the First Baptist Church of Clinton (North Carolina). He has impressed himself upon my estimation as a person with great promise for ministry and larger Christian service. A brilliant mind is coupled with a passion for people and ministry in this young pastor-scholar. He read the manuscript and helped me to know where I had hit and missed the intended marks. He encouraged me with frequent text messages with things to think about, 140 characters at a time. Though he has never studied under my ministry nor has he ever been an associate-in-ministry in any of the places where I have served, I first took to him as a son in ministry. As the days came and went and I learned more of him and he more of me, I took him as a son – whether he likes it or not. That mentor-mentee relationship provides significantly more delight to me than it does to him. I am grateful for his constant forbearance with an old man who is proud of this young pastor's accomplishments and pleased wherever I can see a small hint of myself in him.

The Reverend Jeremy A. Jones was a member and an associate minister in the Temple Memorial Baptist Church in High Point, North Carolina, during the time I was serving as their and his family's pastor. He is now in his first pastorate at the Beaver Dam Baptist Church in Sampson County (North Carolina). When I was his pastor, Jeremy and I spent countless hours together discussing everything from how to craft a good sermon to how to get a good deal on a mortgage for a house to how to best address the inevitable challenges of being a good father, husband and a man. At the time of this writing, he and I found ourselves again residing in close proximity and he was drafted into the work of reviewing this manuscript. Jeremy helped me measure the emotion that my words sought to replicate. He found it funny (when it was supposed to be funny), sad (when it was supposed to be sad) and uplifting (when it was supposed to be uplifting). His assessments made me to know when I was on the right track. I am grateful for the many times that he has, like what the North Star does for a sailor, kept me on the right and best course.

The Reverend Malcolm A. Eatmon is a young minister in my Baptist orbit in North Carolina. He, like me, has an undergraduate degree in English and, at present, juggles ministry and teaching. When I had become weary and worn from searching the pages and paragraphs of this book for grammatical and typographical errors, Reverend Eatmon came to me rescue. He provided the final edit to the manuscript and offered some very meaningful insights as to what meaning was in my words for a minister in the morning of ministry. I suspect he was kinder than the work deserves, but he actually encouraged me to exert the final push to put this work into publication. I owe him (and his last born son, Nathaniel Parker Eatmon) a great debt inasmuch as Reverend Eatmon was reading and working on my manuscript while also attending to his newborn son and devoted wife following Nathaniel's birth.

Dr. Dorwin L. Howard, Sr. found time, amid his many duties as a Superintendent of a North Carolina public school district, to read and react to my manuscript. I have thought of Dorwin as a big brother across the almost thirty years of our friendship. Without question, he likely knows more of my heart than do most people. He was able to assess how true these pages were to the little brother that he has guided, protected, supported, and encouraged across the years. He invited me to tell my story without reservation or second thought. When the subject was difficult, he helped me to measure the weight of embarrassment that might be caused against the possibility of help and hope that this book might offer others. As always, he was right. Always calm and never boisterous, he has the amazing ability of bring calm to my storms and light to my dark pathways. He is the thoughtful and thinking kind of preacher that I have always wanted to be.

My big sister from college, Gloria W. Gosling, was the most excited reader of the early draft of this book. She was the cheerleader that my soul needed! I have told something of her and of our lives in college together, but so much remains untold. I set out to make this book not a re-telling of my life story, but a telling of my ministry. Gloria has been, not only a supporter of my ministry, but a dependable help in life. Life is such that we do not get to see each other as much as either of us would like, but our bond is such that it seems that an absence of months seems to be only a few passing moments. We are always able to pick up just where we left off. I doubt that many people have ever loved me as intentionally and as intently as Gloria has. Warts and all, she has always respected me when I was at my best and pushed me when I was at my lowest. Without her, my life would have not been as sweet and, because of her, my sweet life has been the frame for an amazing ministry. Thank you, Glo!

Dr. James Donald Ballard honored me with writing the preface to this book. I sent the early manuscript to him in hopes that he would read it and offer some small advice. Dr. Ballard took to the manuscript and offered some needed corrections. I thought I was taking a long shot in asking him to write the preface. I was shocked that he so heartily agreed. Without question, Dr Ballard's words are the best part of this book. Each time that I have read his kind words, I have become more and more aware of how blessed my ministry has been with encouragement from giants such as James Donald Ballard. Dr. Ballard has, for the last decade, been given to the ministry of the interim pastorate in North Carolina. Like everything else he has done in life, he has excelled. From time to time, he will call upon me to preach in his stead at one of his interim appointments. I am always careful to tell the gathering that, for more than thirty years, J. D. Ballard has labored to make something out of me. Though he has not succeeded, he has proven to be persistent. I thank him for his persistence in helping me to see this project to publication.

Finally, I need to call the names of my brothers in ministry: The Reverend Dr. Thomas D. Johnson, Sr., The Reverend Dr. Gregory K. Moss, Sr., The Reverend Dr. Greggory Maddox, and (although mentioned previously) The Reverend Dr. Dorwin L. Howard, Sr. These men have guarded my heart and my spirit across the decades with a fierce loyalty and passion. I hope that I have been worthy of their love and devotion. And I hope I have offered some small thing to them in return for all that they have poured into me.